Reality Check

Check

A Common Sense Guide to Breaking into the Music Industry

By

Matthew Walt

MW Global Arts

iUniverse, Inc.

New York   Bloomington

Reality Check
A Common Sense Guide to Breaking
into the Music Industry

iUniverse books may be ordered through booksellers or by contacting:

iUniverse
1663 Liberty Drive
Bloomington, IN 47403
www.iuniverse.com
1-800-Authors (1-800-288-4677)

ISBN: 978-0-595-48782-0 (sc)
ISBN: 978-0-595-51373-4 (hc)
ISBN: 978-0-595-60842-3 (ebook)

Printed in the United States of America

iUniverse rev. date: 1/27/2009

For Emily and Jocelyn

Contents

**Section I - Understanding the Reality of the Business
            Philosophically**

Section II - Building a Business Practically

Acknowledgments

Writing this book has been a long and arduous process—three years in the making and I could probably tweak it ad infinitum, continually adding new chapters and/or editing those included herein. But much like the advice I impart on artists when they enter the recording studio—that there is such a thing as too much, and if you attempt to gloss it over with excessive edits you risk stripping the music of its soul—there came a point at which it just had to be done. Perhaps not surprisingly, I found it is easier to give this advice than to accept it. With that in mind I must acknowledge two things, first and foremost: that I am fully aware, now more than ever, that accepting my suggestions is not something artists will take at face value, but rather something I hope they will take under advisement and find a way to make the adjustments which will work for them; and that my wife is a saint without whom this book wouldn't be possible. For her love, her support, and her constructive criticism—even when I didn't want to hear it—I am eternally grateful.

Also to my parents and brother, for their inspiration as musicians and music educators, among other things; to Howie Cusack, for the knowledge and wisdom he has imparted over the years; to Abbey Parcellin, Julie Viscardi, Emily Mavraganis, Jackie Indrisano, and Jessie Goldbas, for their time, suggestions, encouragement and enthusiasm as this project evolved; to Dalton Sim and Nick Storch, for their very kind words; and to Earl Greyhound, one of my favorite bands (check them out!), for allowing me to use a shadow image of them as my cover, I thank you all very much.

Additionally, to the many musicians and industry professionals with whom I have worked over the years, whether mentioned in this book or not: you have all helped me shape my perspective on the industry, and it has been an absolute pleasure getting to know each and every one of you (even those about whom I might be critical in this book). I cannot imagine what my life would be like if I had chosen another path, nor do I care to.

Finally, to the designers, developers, and contributors to the many free music resources available on the Internet—the Wikipedia community, above all—thank you for helping me fill in the gaps in my mind to communicate what I hope to be accurate information when relating examples throughout this text.

Preface

An Inconvenient Truth about the Music Industry

When I started writing this book in 2006, I came across statistics of record sales from the previous year on a website called AnalogIndustries.com, which, on the one hand, blew my mind, and, on the other, reinforced everything I believe about the best interest of the independent artist. At the time, the labels were in decline. The majority continue to flounder today, the "big four" (Sony BMG, Universal, Warner, and EMI) especially. Nevertheless, the implications of the following statistics remain unchanged.

In 2005, the industry's leading sales-tracking service, Nielsen SoundScan, reported that 60,331 new albums were released by recognized labels (both major and independent), selling a grand total of just over 244 million units.

Out of those 244 million, the majority (169.2 million) were sold by just 410 titles, each of which moved in excess of 100,000 units. The remaining 74.8 million copies therefore constitute the combined total number of sales by the other 59,921 releases—which averages out to a very paltry 1,249 units each!

The overwhelming majority (49,000+) of these releases were put out on small, independent imprints, and that is part of the reason the average figure of 1,249 units each appears so low. The independent releases, after all, averaged fewer than 800 sales apiece that year.

On the other hand, if you subtract the number of sales by those major label releases which sold in excess of 100,000 units, what you discover is that the remaining 10,700 or so major label titles sold an average of barely 3,000 units apiece!

These facts raise some serious questions not just about the state of the record labels but about the industry itself. While it is no secret that the music industry (much like many others) is dependent upon the few at the top sustaining those throughout the ranks, it is a cause for concern that any artist signed to a label would sell 3,000 copies or less in the calendar year of their record's release.

Some will argue that these numbers are directly affected by the growing shift from purchasing entire albums to downloading single songs. There is truth in that statement. Others will say that many releases take longer than the calendar year in which they come out to really connect with an audience. This too, I will not deny. Internet piracy/file sharing by way of P2P (peer-to-peer) software is also a fact of life. However, 3,000 copies by a major label release, and 800 or fewer for an indie—how can that be?

I believe the greater issue involved is the lack of artist development in the industry. My view is not uncommon. But while many attribute this shortcoming to what goes on at the record labels, as if they are solely and completely responsible for this failure, I believe that with all the resources available today the greater responsibility belongs to the artists themselves. The bottom line is: artists need to become educated in the ways of the business and less reliant on others to make sales happen for them. They need to learn how to build a fan base on their own and not fall back on the false sense of security that a label can provide.

Similarly, I believe that there needs to be greater attention paid to professional development—administrative arts education, if you will—at the labels, agencies, management companies, promoters, et al., to insist that all young hires become well rounded and understanding of the big picture early in their careers. We need to educate future generations of music business professionals to respect and appreciate the traditional roles of the various players within the industry while they look for new and different opportunities to expand the boundaries of what they and their artists are capable of doing.

There are labels making strides to improve their business models, and there are independent companies (management firms, in particular) that are helping to build careers the right way. But fixing the structural issues that exist within the industry today is just a temporary solution to a long-term problem, as the technologies employed will continue to evolve, putting even greater strength in the hands of the artists themselves, as well as the professionals who possess the creativity to think differently. By putting the onus back on the individual (artist and professional) and training them to seek out educational experiences, to stay ahead of the curve, and get immersed in the process, we will see as a long-term benefit a happier and healthier industry that continually perpetuates and improves upon itself. This will make success a self-fulfilling prophecy and raise the bar for everyone.

Shaping My Perspective

I come from a family of classical musicians and music educators, so the life of a musician is all I've ever known. I got my start in the business of music at a summer festival called Tanglewood, in 1991. I spent my summers working there while I was in college, and then I went to work in the rock 'n' roll business in 1995 at a small independent label called Rykodisc USA, where I got my hands into anything and everything they permitted, from marketing and publicity to sales and product management. That led to the offer of an agency job thereafter, and since then the majority of my career has been spent at a boutique music business company in Boston, Massachusetts, called Pretty Polly Productions.

Pretty Polly is a company with a long history of identifying and developing talent, and in my time there I have enjoyed a great working relationship with several artists and their representatives, including Gavin DeGraw, Guster, and State Radio, among others. I have also had the great pleasure to produce tours which have featured the likes of All-American Rejects, Howie Day, and Gym Class Heroes (twice). Through each of these attractions, and so many others, I have observed how different artists go about their business in different ways: the interpersonal relations between the various band members, the differing organizational structures, the varying dynamics between their respective business associates—in particular, their agents, managers, tour managers, and production managers.

My focus has always been on the live performance side of the business, save for my eighteen months at Ryko. But I have also been a part of a number of creative marketing initiatives and borne witness to so many more: street-team development programs, logo design competitions, text2win promotions, etc.

However, all of the successful acts with whom I have worked, and all of the well-conceived promotions set in motion to propel an artist's career in the right direction would mean little without proper context, and that is where my unique perspective applies. I have had the distinct pleasure to work with a number of truly talented artists who slugged it out in the trenches for many, many years without ever managing to see the light of day (so to speak). I have booked and consulted some phenomenally gifted musicians who couldn't do some of the little things (and the not-so-little things), which became glaring deficiencies which they simply could not overcome. I have had many late-night conversations with young artists and their "managers" (some deserving of the title and some not so much yet) who believed in their hearts and souls that they were doing everything right, but, for whatever reason, could never get to first base.

I have learned from some of their mistakes. I have made a number of my own (and hopefully learned from them, too). When you see what it's like to be in that trench, wondering if that "deal" (we'll get to that later) will ever come, *that* is when you come to appreciate the blood, sweat, and tears that the biggest of the big have experienced in order to achieve.

I'm not suggesting I am the only one to see things from both sides—most industry professionals have had both successes and failures of their own. But to write from the perspective of the artists in the trench, who are hoping that they can climb out and stand on their own two feet, makes my perspective unique.

There are a number of great books about the music industry, none greater than the "industry bible" by Donald Passman, *All You Need to Know About the Music Business*. These many books provide valuable insight for people who work in the industry, and for those who don't yet, they provide a glimpse of what goes on behind the curtain, should they be so lucky as to find themselves on the other side. However, I do not believe there is a single book out there which provides simple suggestions that artists and aspiring professionals can employ to give themselves the opportunity to break into the music industry and get to the other side of that curtain—until now.

Introduction

There are few among us who have not fantasized about sex, drugs, and rock 'n' roll. Tales of rock 'n' roll excess provide hope and inspiration to millions. And who doesn't like to hear about it? If you dream of having that life, it fuels your existence. If, on the other hand, you abhor that lifestyle, it evokes a passionate response all the same. As for those of you whose feelings lie somewhere in between, it provokes some sensation that keeps your attention nonetheless, as very few are indifferent, no matter what they may say—it's a fact. It's like a train wreck or a car crash on the highway: awful as it may be, traffic backs up for miles as people slow to have a look, to see for themselves, to be a part of the experience in some small way.

That said, if you opened these pages hoping for stories about rock 'n' roll excess, whether for sheer enjoyment or else to add to your personal fantasy files, I'm sorry to say you will be sorely disappointed. (I suggest you instead check out *The Dirt*, the authorized biography of Mötley Crüe as told by the members themselves, or *Stairway to Heaven*, the unauthorized biography of Led Zeppelin told by longtime tour manager Richard Cole.) But if your fascination with the music industry goes beyond the glam, or if perhaps you are an aspiring artist or young professional wondering what it takes to catch a break, I'd like to believe you have come to the right place.

I warn you, however—all you artists with your big dreams of big houses, fast cars, beautiful women, and the adoration of millions—the following chapters might be a rude awakening, the kick in the pants that you have been avoiding for years, and the bursting of the bubble in which you'd prefer to spend the rest of your life.

Of course, if you've really got what it takes to prove the naysayers wrong, I respect your sincerity and have hope you take the good in what I say and recognize that it comes from a positive place.

First, let's put things into perspective. An overwhelming number of artists on this planet never fully realize their dreams. Most don't even get to first base. For every story about excess, for every VH1 *Behind the Music*, for every episode of MTV *Cribs*, there are tens of millions who gave it a try and failed. And while most of our mothers tell us we can be anything we want to be, and while every artist believes his or her music—or painting, or sculpture, or book—is absolutely mind-blowing, the odds remain that most of us won't even have the privilege of a cameo on another personal favorite: VH1's *Where Are They Now?*

You may be saying to yourself, "But what about so-and-so? She absolutely sucks! If she can do it, I can too!" Or you might say, "What do you mean it's going to take years of my life, working my ass off, 24-7, 365, just to get my foot in the door? Such and such was an overnight success! I heard they formed on Tuesday and had a record deal by Thursday afternoon!"

Well, I'm sorry to say there's usually a pretty good reason that you might be overlooking for why so-and-so can do it, and it's more than a little bit likely that such and such worked harder than you think. After all, it takes a special kind of person with a special set of skills and a special team around them to get successful music business professionals lining up for the opportunity to drool over him or her—no matter what you may have heard.

What's more, just because you are the recipient of some well-deserved drool does not guarantee your place in history. Oh no—success is not the almighty deal, or the support slot on the groundbreaking national tour. No, no—the big break is not the be-all and end-all. The *break* that you seek, that I write about, is what I like to call *sea level*. It is the point at which you have earned the opportunity to make a living doing what you've always dreamed of. Unfortunately, that means—to all of you working a day job, dreaming about the good life, feeling like you've already paid your dues—that right now you are just learning to tread water and are gasping for air. And like my eighth-grade science teacher, Mr. Henriques, always said, "If you are below C level, then you are drowning."

Depressed yet? I hope not. Prepared to work harder than you ever imagined for considerably less than the government-recognized minimum wage? You'd better be, because it doesn't have to be that way forever. Just because the deck is stacked against you, it does not mean that it's not worth a shot. Everybody deserves a shot. I believe that wholeheartedly—just as I believe that everybody has the potential to succeed. Unfortunately, most people don't know how to tap into that potential. And even among those who do, many do not put forth the effort that is necessary to realize their dreams.

But here's the good news: Success in rock 'n' roll requires no degree. Intelligence, yes; business savvy, I'd say so, if only to recognize your personal limitations and who you can trust—but not necessarily a college degree. Of course, there are several highly accredited music (and music business) schools that will offer them—and I'm not saying they aren't worth consideration. But, as with anything taught in schools, regardless of the discipline, classroom learning doesn't always prepare you for the real world, and in the arts this is especially true.

Of course, I don't claim to be an expert. I have no theory, I know no scientific method, I have never studied rocket science, and I could not perform brain surgery. But I do have common sense. And my experience has taught me that in the business of music, common sense is all that you need. Common sense is your best friend, your most dangerous weapon, and your most valuable asset.

The book is broken down into five sections. The first is a philosophical approach to understanding the business, both inside and out: the dream and the reality; the strength of self, the spirit, and the mental stability required (however ironic that would seem); and the passion with which you must conduct your business, both onstage and off, to give people a sense of who you are, what you represent, and why they should take you into their hearts, their minds, and their daily routines.

The second section is all about building your small business, because the music itself may be a simple matter of personal expression, but exposing it to the world requires a plan. There must be a course of action in order to designate responsibility, identify and promote to your fans, and develop your reputation while you are learning how to adapt and understand the industry in which you hope to make a living.

The third section details several tried-and-true methods for presenting yourself in the press and on site, on record, and onstage to garner the most positive attention. It is a road map to ingratiating yourself appropriately and tapping your potential just by being you.

Sections four and five fuse the philosophical and theoretical approaches that help you to fine-tune your skills and appreciate the value of doing it yourself to further your cause in the long run, should you be so fortunate as to make it to the next level.

I do not have all of the answers, but I do know many of the problem areas from having stumbled upon them myself or by observing others. Hopefully, the information contained within these pages will help you avoid some of the more common mistakes by using your good sense to make the right decisions, which will lead to the many breaks that you are going to need to make your dreams come true. So please, turn the page. I wish you the best of luck.

This is your reality check.

Section I

Understanding the Reality of the Business Philosophically

Dream Big

> When I was a Beatle, I thought we were the best goddamn group in the goddamn world ... and believing that is what made us what we were. It was just a matter of time before everybody else caught on.
>
> —John Lennon

> Imagination is more important than knowledge.
>
> —Albert Einstein

I am a believer in big dreams. Clichéd as it may seem, the concept, "If you can dream it you can achieve it" really does ring true to me. It is imperative to see something in your mind and believe it is possible if you really want to make it happen. For instance, Marilyn Manson didn't become Marilyn Manson by accident. Axl, Slash, Duff, Izzy—Guns N' Roses was more than just a random collection of guys. Look at KISS: the makeup, the costumes—what a concept! And Eminem, aka Slim Shady, aka Marshall Mathers—all are ideas, manifested in artistry, which shaped their respective persona, provoked thought, and evoked an emotional response from onlookers, thereby fueling their existence and making their dreams come true.

I remember, on VH1's *Behind the Music*, Bret Michaels, of the group Poison, talking about what the members went through. To me, that was the ultimate episode in the series—the one that really exemplified the struggles of becoming rock 'n' roll superstars. They moved to LA without two pennies to rub together, all of them living in a tiny rat-infested apartment, not knowing where their next meal was coming from—all the while working their asses off every day putting up flyers for their upcoming concerts and carefully crafting their glamorous vagabond image in order to work their way into the hearts and minds of America's youth. Perhaps I'm giving them too much credit, but do you really think a debut album called *Look What the Cat Dragged In* happened by accident?

Dreams becoming reality is a universal concept that extends far beyond music. Think of the pyramids in Egypt, the Taj Mahal, the life's work of Leonardo da Vinci. It takes a larger-than-life vision to become larger than life. Consider U2: Bono's messianic complex—the enthusiasm and devotion with which he goes about his business on and offstage—is part of what makes him arguably the most noteworthy figure in rock 'n' roll today (if not ever). And despite his seemingly soft-spoken nature, fellow U2 mate The Edge does call himself "The Edge," which sounds a whole lot more rock 'n' roll than if he went by his given name: David Evans.

Of course, it's not just about creating a character, and the intention need not be world domination in order to affect people's lives. Bob Dylan is nothing if not true to himself and insistent on pleasing no one, yet his music speaks to generations of people and breathes life into the ideals they uphold. His understanding of the world, and his place within it, has allowed him to create music that is both groundbreaking and influential. Take, for example, his famed performance at the Newport Folk Festival in 1965, where he broke out his electric guitar and forever changed the world of folk music. To be fair, on that day Dylan alienated a portion of his fan base that had certain expectations of what his music should be, and in the short term that may not have been such a good thing. Yet, by pushing the limit and challenging the expectations of his fans, in hindsight one might say that on that day Dylan cemented his legacy as an advocate for change, reflected in his word and his deed, both in art and in life.

Few attain great success purely by accident. Even those artists who insist that the music found them (many artists, in all disciplines, refer to their gifts with great humility, as if they are simply a medium) typically possess and employ their ability to communicate in a way that evokes an idea or an image in order to connect with an audience.

No one dreams of living in a shithole apartment—dirty, starving, wearing secondhand clothes—because mediocrity and a substandard living situation is what they aspire to. Well, almost no one—there are invariably exceptions to every rule. But the point is that the dream is the first step in realizing who you are and what you want to be. So, be proud of your dream, embrace your dream, and believe in your ability to make it come true. If you can do that, you have taken the first step in fulfilling your rock 'n' roll fantasy.

So You Want to Be in a Band

If you are like me, the notion of a "real job" sounds like a fate worse than death—sitting in a cubicle, surrounded by corporate suits, doing "the nine-to-five thing" as your life passes you by. Who among us spent their childhood dreaming of wasting their life away seated behind a desk? I certainly didn't. But then, strangely, that is what I do much of the time, even though I work in entertainment—and so does just about everyone else I know.

You may think: what better way to escape a life of dread than to join a band? Perhaps you started while in high school because you had a passion for the Beatles, the Cure, or the Crüe. Maybe you got into it later in life for the ladies, the free booze, the camaraderie, or the escape. If you are a hobbyist, then more power to you. A passion for music is a passion for life, and future generations will be better off for it. But if you are in a band because you want to "make it big," whether you think in terms of superstardom or just to eke out a living doing something other than that lousy desk job, then it starts with a simple question: *Do you really have what it takes?*

Before you answer with a resounding YES, ask yourself one more: *Do you really know what that means?*

The problem, in my experience, is that most people forget to ask themselves that second question. They are so sure they have the talent that they overlook, or ignore—or worse, take for granted—the work which makes the requisite exposure possible.

Writing popular music is easy, they think. "My songs could stand alongside anything on the radio," artists tell me *all the time*. "The music is there—I just need someone to handle the business," they say to themselves and anyone else who will listen.

They spend hundreds, sometimes thousands, of dollars—whether their own or someone else's—creating expensive press kits with elaborate bios, and a full-length CD with eighteen songs, because every single one of them just needed to be on there—they're all really just that good (or so they say)! They send these kits to everyone whose contact info they've ever collected: agents, managers, record labels, clubs, colleges, festivals—you name it.

There is an old saying that if you throw enough shit against a wall some of it will stick. Certainly there is an element of truth to that notion. But I don't buy into that line of thinking in regard to artist promotion. To me, that's just a waste of time and money. However, to an unknowing artist, a mass solicitation can feel like an achievement in itself. After all, you are spending time and money doing the things that you think you are supposed to do: putting your music in the hands of the maximum number of people. It's a reasonable conclusion to make—and goes along with the belief that if you are constantly doing everything you can then sooner or later something is going to happen.

However, before you spend your life savings or max out all your credit cards, consider whether or not there is a better use of your time and money. Ask yourself if it might make more sense to be doing *the right things* versus anything and everything. Try to determine if it is really worth sending an elaborate press kit and your full-length CD to people who may never see them. In time, you may find you aren't making the headway that you could be, no matter how much effort and money you expend.

So let's slow it down for a moment and start to outline a plan by asking a series of questions, such as:

What are your goals and objectives—both short-term and long?

What do you hope to achieve? A record deal? A hit song? A career on the road?

Who is your target audience? Are you able to identify a particular demographic?

How are you going to reach them? Are there specific Web sites
or blogs you can utilize?
Who else caters to that audience?
How have they been successful?
What specific steps did they take?
How much time do you have available to you?
How should you structure that time?
What are your assets?
Who are your partners?
What are your strengths and weaknesses?
What relationships would be of value to you and why?
How do you cultivate those relationships in the first place?
How do you foster those relationships over time?

Asking (and answering) all of these questions and structuring your
business accordingly will help distinguish you from your competition—
and whether your business is a band, a booking agency, or a bread
company, it just might give you a chance. Of course, in doing so, what
you will inevitably find is that you are right where you thought you
never wanted to be: seated behind a desk, working regular hours—at
least for the time being.

The Notion of the Big, Bad Industry

> The music business is a cruel and shallow money trench, a long plastic hallway where thieves and pimps run free and good men die like dogs. There's also a negative side.

This quote is widely associated with Hunter S. Thompson, but he never actually said it. Rather, it is a paraphrase of a reference he once made to the television industry. Nevertheless, the sentiment has taken on a life of its own, as it is commonly considered to be true.

There is a notion that the industry is filled with criminals—that there are always people out to get you. That may or may not be true. There are shady characters in every industry, and the music business is no exception. So I would advise all to be diligent and methodical in everything you do, no matter what the circumstance. But the suggestion that the music industry is different from the rest is really an exaggeration. Perhaps there are fewer professionals with advanced degrees. Admittedly, there are several with no degrees at all. After all, there are relatively few music business schools, and, frankly, the industry is just not set up that way. Regardless, I say whether you become a predator or prey is sometimes just a matter of perspective.

Agents think venues and promoters screw them all the time, and vice versa. Artists think labels take every advantage, and perhaps there are those that do.

There was a time when those in power did prey on all those beneath them—or so the stories have been told. The great R & B stars of the

50s and 60s and the great songwriters of yesteryear have legitimate grievances when they say they got scammed out of millions in royalties. But in today's music industry the notion that every club owner, agent, manager, and record executive is just a two-bit criminal is really not the case. In most instances when one party feels victimized by another, it's really just a matter of one business person knowing more. For instance, if an artist doesn't know how to cut a good deal, that doesn't mean that the talent buyer is a con man. That a manager knows he can take 30 percent of all proceeds from the artist whose career he's helped create doesn't necessarily make him a fraud.

I don't mean to suggest that people who know how to manipulate the system are necessarily good business people. Rather, I mean to reinforce the simple proposition that a little bit of knowledge can go a long way—and that by learning the ropes and understanding the game, one can learn how to avoid being victimized. And if the time comes that you discover that you have been cheated, you might want to reassess. It's like the saying goes: "Fool me once, shame on you. Fool me twice, shame on me." Or something along those lines ...

The reality, in my experience, is that the industry is filled with well-intentioned, good business people who are constantly expanding their minds and learning about new and different things in order to better their own careers. As these professionals adopt more efficient and more profitable methods of doing their jobs, the best and brightest always rise to the top.

My point is: educate yourself in the process. If you don't go to school then read a book, listen to stories, and get a grasp of your situation. Try to see things from outside yourself—who you are, where you fit in, and what you must do to advance your position. Do this and the criminals will (usually) be easy to avoid, and the right decisions will be obvious to all. What you choose to do then is entirely up to you, but at least you'll be equipped to decide.

If you choose to ignore this advice, then enter the business at your own peril, for it is because of people like you that these thieves are able to thrive.

Don't Quit Your Day Job

Now that you've formulated a plan, the next step must be quitting your day job and committing 100 percent of your energy to your career in music, right? WRONG! As logical as it might seem, it's unlikely that your business is thriving to the point that you can afford to focus on it full time just yet. Even if you've got the time, or don't need to make money due to the blessing of independent wealth, it's still unlikely that your business *requires* that you spend your days sitting at the computer, or in the studio, or hitting the streets in the early development stages. *This is not to imply that you should not be practicing and rehearsing as much as you can.*

I'm not suggesting that you should be finding other ways to waste your time if you have enough to spare. But a band is like a great roast that needs to marinate, or a gravy that needs time to simmer. You can't just add water and expect the finished product to be as good as if it were made from scratch.

All good things take time. A great hook might grab you and sweep you off your feet, but it's unlikely to happen right away. If it does, it does—it's happened before: the first time you heard John Lennon's "Imagine," or Public Enemy's "Fight the Power." There are songs throughout history that make an immediate impression. Nevertheless, ninety-nine times out of a hundred, it didn't happen overnight. In fact, ninety-nine times out of a hundred, it didn't happen at all.

Consider the band Maroon 5, who toured behind their brilliant 2002 release, *Songs About Jane*, for well over a year—some say it took two—before they really reached the tipping point (see Malcolm

Gladwell's *The Tipping Point* for reference—more on that later), and their first single, "Harder to Breathe" went global. But what's most remarkable about Maroon 5 is that four of the five original members originally formed back in 1995, under the name Kara's Flowers. That's right: 1995! It took Maroon 5—arguably the most hooky pop band of the early twenty-first century—ten years in order to be awarded the title Best New Artist at the 2005 Grammys.

Think about that.

Don't Start Paying Yourself Just Yet

Let's say you have enacted a plan that is starting to take shape. You are gigging regularly, somewhere between four and ten times per month, and it feels like things are starting to gel. The audiences are growing steadily, mostly by word of mouth. You've got a good Web presence, you are garnering positive attention, and people in the industry are starting to take your calls.

Of course, most of the venues you are playing still double as restaurants, and the guy eating buffalo wings four feet from the stage is not exactly everything that you'd hoped and dreamed your audience would be, BUT you are getting paid more than enough to cover your fuel costs, and that means everyone can get a taste, right?

Well, you could do that. Certainly, paying yourselves every once in a while makes you feel like a professional. A professional! But again, let's slow down and think this through for a moment. What is it that the band really needs right now? Your monthly overhead is probably still low: a rehearsal space, Web hosting fees, a van, which also requires insurance, and a slush fund in the event of a breakdown on the side of the road. But that's about all—and it leaves you with a little bit of spare change, so why not spread it around? Here are just a few considerations that you might want to bear in mind before doing so:

- Unless a record deal is imminent, you might need to pay for studio time again one day soon. That may or may not include the cost of a decent producer and engineer.

13

- Once the new gem is recorded, you may want to mix and master it. That isn't cheap.
- Every performance merits a quality promotion. If you ever really want to draw, you need to start printing flyers, posters, stickers and the like—anything that can help you brand your product (see "Brand Marketing" in Section II).
- New merchandise costs money too, and while you hope it'll pay for itself, vendors usually require an up-front payment.
- There are countless industry conferences and festivals that are definitely worth your while in your quest for knowledge and contacts throughout the industry. These events vary by price, and their validity to your specific circumstances are worth taking into account, but South By Southwest, CMJ, NACA, MEISA, the many Billboard conferences, Pop Montreal, and many more are all worth consideration.

These are just a few of the reasons that you might want to open a savings account rather than divvying up whatever surplus you make at the shows. Of course, if music is your livelihood and that money really does make a difference, then far be it from me to suggest you forgo it. But if you can spare it, your band can use it. And believe me—it makes a difference in the end.

Time to Burst the Bubble

Look, if you had one shot, or one opportunity
To seize everything you ever wanted—one moment
Would you capture it or just let it slip?

—Eminem, "Lose Yourself"

Now it's time to burst the bubble. You're gigging regularly, everything is going according to plan, and you understand that quitting your day job is not in the cards just yet, nor is getting rich and living large like you see on MTV's *Cribs*. But you *are* inching closer to realizing your dream and it's really starting to feel like it could happen.

Well don't get me wrong, because it could. But before you go and buy that three-thousand-dollar guitar that is guaranteed to take your sound to the next level, it's time that you understand the reality of the business: in all likelihood your band is never going to make it. It's not that it can't, but odds are it won't.

The bottom line is that most small businesses fail—not just in music, but in life. Forget the stats—the variance from study to study on rates of failure are all over the map, and they are irrelevant to our discussion. If you've spent enough time in the trenches, playing the club scene and socializing with other artists, then you know that most bands fold long before they ever achieve a small taste of success. That doesn't mean you should stop trying. But the odds are not in your favor, and I think that is worth noting. I say this not to drag you down, but to inspire you, to fuel your passion, and to compel you to work that much harder than you ever have before so that you are *always* forging ahead, *always* chipping away, and *always* inching closer, even just a little bit, *every* day. If you can do that, then you will increase the possibility that will defy the statistics which are heavily stacked against you.

Over the years I've noticed an element of complacency that seems to occur among young aspiring rockers when they feel that they are onto something good. The moment they realize that what they are doing is starting to work, that the music is strong, and the attention is coming—all of a sudden they feel it is time to relax and allow someone else to pick up the slack. I can appreciate that logic—you feel that you are close enough to slow it down, take a breath, and bring on additional support so that you can focus completely on the music. Unfortunately, however, the opposite reaction may prove more likely to benefit you in the long term: *When you reach the point that what you are doing is paying off, it's time to work harder and push yourself more, both onstage and off.*

One of the most talented artists I ever worked with is a singer/ songwriter from Colorado, whom I'll call RJ, whose story is equal parts sad and a product of his own poor decision making. In the 1990s he was the leader of a band signed to Capricorn Records. His revolving cast of backup musicians featured the likes of T-Bone Wolk and Kenny Aronoff on one of his records, and the great Graham Nash actually did a duet with him on another. Yet the story goes (as I was not yet working with him then) that on the day of his first major label release, his manager was actually on vacation!

Imagine that—the biggest moment of a young artist's life, when all hands should be on deck working tirelessly to make sure that the first impression he makes is the absolute best it can be, and the manager is sitting on a beach!

Don't get me wrong—the band experienced modest success, in that they toured for several years, sold 50,000+ copies, went through two record deals, changed their name, then changed it back, and RJ made enough money to buy a house—all of which is more than most bands can say. But, in truth, they never broke through. The size of the venues they headlined never exceeded theatres, and in time they returned to the club level. RJ cared only about the music, allowing everything to be taken care of by others, never caring for the business side of it himself. That's all well and good—I can't fault him for his choice—but, in the end, that left no one else to blame when the day came that it was over, what little money they had made had dried up, and the band simply faded away.

I got the call through RJ's publicist when the decision was made to go solo. I knew some of the band's history, but believing the guy to be unbelievably talented, I leapt. Unfortunately, the infusion of fresh blood and the momentum that comes with a "debut" wore off in a short time. It soon became apparent that this fabulous, but now aging, singer/songwriter was just a little too set in his ways to make significant strides to further his opportunities, not to mention the fact that his lack of business acumen left something to be desired.

He had a handful of rabid fans, but no viral marketing initiative. He was willing to co-write with other songwriters, but attending concerts and networking with other artists of his stature was not his idea of a good time. He did the festival circuit but made no lasting impressions. He wanted everything on his own terms. He preferred the small, intimate venues where he could command attention—a decision with which I happened to agree. However, he could only fill a couple of those nationwide, and he would have to play many more, for very little money, repeatedly for several years to develop any kind of following. I never got the impression he was willing to do that.

RJ was never quite willing to go the extra mile to push himself over the top. I determined that he'd become used to disappointment and maintained very low expectations. Whether that contributed to his general sadness (another facet of his personality I became aware of along the way) or if it was the other way around, it took its toll on me over a couple of years, as I felt like I was the only one putting him out there.

I've kept an eye on RJ in the years since. I believe he does take care of his own business now, but that means little in the way of activity. He's been offered a few decent gigs, but they don't seem to translate to anything bigger and better. I receive his newsletter every once in a while, but it's typically just a listing of his upcoming performance dates. There are no special promotions or exciting opportunities which suggest upward mobility. He seems content to play all of his usual haunts, making the small pockets of fans he's got aware of his goings-on, but never really pushing himself further. I hope one day he gets the credit his music deserves, but his lack of interest in the business makes that possibility remote.

There are those who say that it's all about the music. But without the knowledge and ability, or the motivation, to expose it, an independent artist doesn't have much of a chance, no matter how good the music is. For RJ, in my opinion, that's clearly the case.

RJ's bubble was burst a long time ago, but when it broke, I think it broke his spirit too—that, or it went on vacation. Either way, the point is you should neither fall victim to the same sad ending by switching to cruise control just when things start getting good, nor assume that the music will take care of itself, or that someone will take care of it for you. Burst the bubble now, of your own choice, and give yourself a fighting chance. Don't expect things to be done for you—make them happen for yourself. I have always maintained the opinion that the harder you work, the more you should want to work even harder; and the more success you experience, the more you should want to experience even greater success; and the more you can do all on your own, the more rewarding it will be in the end. Earn that taste of success if you can. Don't let it slip away by assuming it will sustain or by expecting someone will preserve it for you.

The 3 Ps: Patience, Persistence, and Perseverance

Getting ahead of yourself is a natural tendency when you want something very badly, but overlooking some of the steps in a sequence of events may leave you unprepared for what awaits. Whether the result of a perceived inability to advance on your own accord, or else by virtue of a staunch affirmation that you deserve to be further along, the desire to sign with an agent, a manager, or a label all too often consumes an artist long before he or she is ready—and without a real appreciation of what this step means. Regardless, there comes a time in the lives of many young artists, ensembles, and people in all walks of life that enough is enough already—the time has come, you've taken your lumps, you've paid your dues, and you are ready for what's next. All you want is to play in front of an appreciative audience and have everything else handled for you.

You take all those long rides in your beat-up old van, which you've affectionately named something repugnant after an incident not to be repeated in mixed company. You travel day and night to one dive bar after the next in those out-of-the-way college towns that you have heard "really rage"—but they don't on the nights that you're there. Yet you go back, again and again, because you believe it will turn around. And you go further and further away, because you're certain you'll find that feeling somewhere.

You know the feeling: the rush you get when you take the stage and you give it your all and the people GET IT. I'm not talking about the stadium-size crowds that go wild at the sight of you. You long for that too, but most nights all you want is for the twenty-seven people in the five-hundred-capacity club, half of whom work there and the rest of whom might be regulars, to at least pay attention for a portion of your set, to acknowledge your presence when you finish your songs, to avoid the tendency to yell out "Free Bird!" and to tell you afterward that you didn't suck. Because, let's be honest: those nights are all too familiar to most bands that roam the planet like traveling vagabonds.

Even the best have had these experiences on more nights than one. You try to keep that in mind. But when those awful nights occur again and again, on consecutive nights, after long rides in the van, when you don't know where you'll sleep … you reach the point where you say to yourself, "I can't do this anymore. I've paid my f*ing dues. If it doesn't happen soon, then maybe it's time I walk away."

I get it. I understand. It's a perfectly reasonable way of thinking. It's not about entitlement—that's another issue. It's the feeling that you are ready, that it's time; that you shouldn't have to wait another day. To an extent, it's healthy to feel that way. Confidence is important. Believing in yourself is an imperative. It gets you through the day and hopefully has a positive effect on your performance capabilities, as you need to feel good about what you are doing to make others feel good about it too. It's not arrogance, mind you—that can be the death of an artist—but a strong, positive sense of self.

The truth of the matter is that these experiences and these feelings are what most artists go through on a regular basis. That's hardly a comfort, but it's true. Maybe you should walk away. Odds are you won't succeed, right? But before you throw in the towel, remember the three Ps: patience, persistence, and perseverance. They are critical to any great achievement.

Patience is a gift with which I, for one, was not born, but which I was forced to learn the hard way. Patience is everything in the music business, where nothing happens quickly—even for those who have "made it." Records get shelved for months, sometimes years, for artists big and small. Contracts with sponsors, promoters, and labels—these things take time to get right. Then there's the game called Hurry Up and

Wait. "Hurry up and send that package," says the talent buyer. "Then follow up with me in three weeks." Three weeks, of course, quickly becomes three months for the young band, but that's the way it goes. "Hurry up and send that offer," says the agent. "You gotta get it in if your date has any life." But don't expect an answer for at least a week or two. To the independent artist and industry professional dreaming of the big break, patience truly is a virtue, as weeks become months, and months become years. Sometimes it seems like it's working, and people are coming around. But sometimes it seems like people couldn't care less, and maybe the detractors were right. Who really knows what will come in the end—but for now, the wait is just killing you.

Persistence is an absolute imperative. See "Living in the Gray" in Section II. To succeed, you have to be determined. Just because you leave someone a message does not mean that you have fulfilled your duty, and now it's their responsibility to call you back. You are the one who wants something from them, not the other way around. They have a routine of their own, which does not necessarily leave time to return all of the calls they receive. But that does not mean they don't have you in mind should an appropriate opportunity arise; nor does it suggest they are disrespecting you by purposefully ignoring your call. If you show them that you are willing to work for something (whatever it is that you seek to find out), sooner or later they will come around, and you'll get what it is that you are after: sometimes that's a booking, sometimes that's getting someone to see your band play, sometimes that's feedback one way or the other, and sometimes it's closure and nothing more.

Perseverance is what keeps you going when your patience wears thin and persistence doesn't seem to be enough. It's the need to keep going—sings Ben Harper, "The Will to Live." Perseverance comes from deep down inside, from the pit of your stomach or the back of your head or somewhere else within. It fuels your passions in the face of adversity; makes you steadfast and unyielding. It must—because it takes a great love to succeed, an intensity beyond all else. Knowledge only carries you so far, and after that there is that nagging sensation in your gut: a love of the game and an overwhelming urge to make something happen. That's when you persevere, even when the overriding notion is that it simply is not meant to be. Usually, that's when it happens. Things turn around because you stick it out, always believing that everything will work itself out if you let it—and by *letting it* I mean doing every last little thing to ensure that your patience, persistence, and perseverance pay off because that's the only result you will accept.

Everything Takes Longer than You Think

When you finally realize that everything truly does take longer than you think that it should, there are a number of tendencies and potentially harmful habits that certain artists exhibit which you will want to avoid. Among the most challenging to overcome is rash decision making, and the general expression of frustration that can cloud judgment and cause you to lose sight of the reason that you got into music in the first place.

Rash decision making is among the fastest ways to lead your career astray. Jumping into a relationship with the first agent, manager, or label to express interest—without understanding the implications, without knowing whether it's a good fit, and without seeing whether you have other options—is not a good idea. This can happen when you want something so badly you just might convince yourself that *someone* is better than *no one*, and that the *appearance* of a team is better than the *quality* of that team, or that the act of *doing* and the satisfaction it brings are as valuable as doing things *the right way*.

I worked with a reggae/soul singer once upon a time, an incredibly talented young man who I'll call Terrence. He possessed the all-powerful *it* factor—his charisma was unmistakable. When he took the stage, audiences were like putty in his hands. He had a power and a charm that would have made him a star—perhaps they still will; I have faith and he's got time. Unfortunately, however, he had a tendency to rush into things. He went through three managers in a little more than a year—he just wanted so badly for "big things" to happen. He'd meet a young woman at a show who would say she wanted to help, and the next day he'd appoint her his publicist. He received an offer to have his debut CD done free, so he jumped into that situation too, without regard for the fact that he'd have to give up his masters, and without considering the possibility that the producer might be a bad fit. His intentions were always the best—right down to the day he aligned with a former gang banger with several years left on his prison term because the guy offered him "credibility," or so he believed—and that was a potential difference maker in his career.

With the best of intentions, Terrence focused solely on the good in the people with whom he worked. But he failed to recognize that activity in and of itself isn't necessarily what propels an artist forward. So when it was suggested that he needn't move so fast, that time and a thorough review of all options might prove more fruitful in the end, he'd say, "Hey—this train is moving forward. Either you're on it, or you get left behind." But, in time he began to see, sadly, that these decisions were getting him nowhere. In fact, they'd set him back. That's when the questions started to creep into his mind, and the negativity followed soon after, as he wondered whether it was worth all of the hassle.

Frustration is another potential career killer that rears its head for so many young artists. A promoter friend of mine often speaks of encounters with young artists who become irate when they don't receive calls back from him. They are unaware that he works tirelessly to run a small business and hasn't the time for everyone who calls. They are inconsiderate of the fact that he has the heart to offer suggestions on his voice message for how specifically to get his attention, in hopes that they will understand and comply. They fail to consider that perhaps he does know who they are and might be keeping them in mind. They disregard the fact that his success depends on making the artists with whom he works successful too. Some of these young bands who have taken none of his advice leave nasty voice messages on his answering machine, saying what a jerk he is for not taking them seriously and how much he will live to regret it! Then they say nasty things, which have no merit, via Internet blogs. But they do it anyway, and in the process they burn a bridge, purely out of frustration.

Similarly, my friend Sam, a record executive, will tell stories about artists who become frustrated with him when he doesn't give them the "respect" they deserve. They tell him that he should be a little more considerate when he speaks to them, because they are trying to help his career. (That, by the way, is my absolute favorite thing to hear—it just kills me every time an artist says they are giving *me* an opportunity to advance *my* career by working with them, because they can help me. More on that later.)

The worst thing about rushing to judgment, jumping into bad (or ill-conceived) situations, and allowing frustration to get the best of you as an artist, is that it can result in getting caught up in your own negativity and losing sight of what fuels your passion in the first place. Never forget what caused you to pick up your instrument and play when you were young, when it wasn't about money, or business, or fame; and it wasn't about the almighty deal. It was fun. It was exciting. You made music for the sake of it, before you became callous and cold, and the business seemingly tainted the process. The problem that results from such negativity, beyond a lack of interest in playing the game, is that your audience is going to know it. If you're not having fun, they're not having fun—and that's when you know it is over.

Don't be burdened by the time that it takes to advance your career. Make the most of it, and keep your chin up. I still believe in Terrence. In time, he may succeed. He just needs to accept the fact that everything takes longer than he thinks.

Passion Over Perfection

Hip-hop is a culture about which I'm no authority, but it serves as an appropriate example to demonstrate my next point. All I know is that a great beat is a great beat, and great poetry is great poetry, regardless of pretense or genre. But much like jazz and blues, hip-hop rose from the streets, representing urban life in its authenticity. I'm not talking about the clutter that commercial radio spins today—where certain artists and producers often perpetuate stereotypes for profit. I'm talking about the root (not The Roots, but them, too)—the foundation upon which an empire has grown, an empire which serves as a great example of a prolific musical art form that was born out of a homegrown means—a homegrown need, one might say—reminding us all where art begins.

Hip-hop grew because MCs, DJs, instrumentalists, entrepreneurs, and fans alike had a passion—one which represented a lifestyle as much as an art form. Read up on The Last Poets, who some say started it all by reading poetry set to percussion, later adding jazz and funk instrumentalists. Research the Holy Trinity of hip-hop: Kool Herc, Afrika Bambaataa, and Grandmaster Flash, who are credited with originating the style of break-beat DJing. Check out the trendsetters who worked both in front of and behind the scenes: The Cold Crush Brothers, The Fatback Band, Tuff City Records, Tommy Boy, and Russell Simmons and Rick Rubin who started Def Jam Recordings in a college dorm.

Before there were big budgets for studio recordings, there were live tapes and four-track recordings. Artists took their craft to block parties, parks, and battles. People got it, because it represented something raw, inspirational, and above all, true. It wasn't about glitz and glamour; it was about politics and fun. It was the embodiment of something real.

These same qualities can be found in the music of major artists of all genres throughout the ages. I highlight hip-hop first and foremost on account of its power as a game changer, in spite of its youth, in the landscape of modern music. But similar examples of current artists in other genres who have taken a raw, low-budget approach include Bright Eyes, the anti-pop singer/songwriter; Dashboard Confessional, who made "emo" cool; The Go! Team, whose debut *Thunder, Lightning, Strike* I consider to be the ultimate low-budget indie pop-rock record; and Iron and Wine, whose sleepy time basement tapes made him a star by accident, according to some accounts. These artists are remarkable for having started as the brainchildren of individuals who took a purely original approach to creating something that reflected who they were and what they stood for by simple means, flaws and all. They succeeded, not in spite of, but because of their simplistic approach, and because originality is born out of a passion to represent one's own truth.

People have flaws. Art needn't be perfect. At times in the modern popular music culture, that can be forgotten. So many artists think that all it takes is enough money to disguise their faults or transform them into something they are not. They overdub their mistakes, again and again; they blend their sounds until they resemble someone they think they ought to be. They mix and remix, smoothing over the rough spots until they gleam, unintentionally stripping away the very essence of the message that was intended to be sent in the first place.

I'm not knocking the recording process, nor am I denouncing the potential beauty of commercially viable popular music. I believe in the value of a great mix, the need to master one's work so that it sounds just right, the desire to dub and overdub—and the possibilities that can result. And frankly, I love a great pop song too.

What I am saying is that money doesn't buy quality music. Worse, the unfortunate and unintended consequence is overproduction, which is the tendency to strip a song of its soul in the quest to get it "right," or make something "perfect," by using studio techniques to "correct" one's shortcomings.

True fans are drawn to imperfection. True fans gravitate toward artists who make music which represents who they are and who they aspire to be. True fans love the anti-pop songs: the ones that weren't overdone; the ones that were never intended to be shopped around or used as singles, so they weren't beaten to death or overscrutinized. These are often the tracks which "fill out" the record—or become outtakes, B sides, or hidden tracks. I'm not talking about the songs that were picked up off the cutting room floor because the record needed to be eight minutes longer. I'm talking about the songs that show another side of an artist's personality, and, as a result, they maintain their integrity. Fans take to these tracks because they represent a greater truth. Yet, too many artists shy away from the music that best reflects the essence of their being—forgetting (or dismissing) the place from which their inspiration was derived—in favor of music which they believe will be more widely accepted. As a result they fail to make their mark.

I believe the pioneers of hip-hop knew that people were starved for truth and inspiration, and they kept it raw, not just by necessity, but in recognition of that fact. To represent the truth is to let it all hang out— the raw, intense, emotional undercurrent that exists beneath the surface and inspires people to do great things—and when they capture their passion on reel or on tape, then there is no need for studio wizardry to overshadow the finished product because passion always wins over perfection. I hope more young artists will keep that in mind.

Section II

Building a Business Practically

Innovation and Initiative

While the focus of this collection appears to be on artists and industry professionals who fulfill traditional roles (agent, manager, etc), it has equal application to those with a vision, the skills, and the initiative to innovate and fulfill nontraditional roles as well. From *MySpace* to *YouTube* to *Facebook* and so on, innovation abounds online—and evolving technologies continue to expand the industry and make room for those with unique and superior computer skills. But what about those who do not possess a high level of computer proficiency?

Here is a sampling of random vocations with application to the music business:

- **Photographer**: Beyond the obvious possibility of photo-journalism, how about creating a business photographing artists in concert? You might trail an artist who is on tour and create a tour photo book.
- **Architect**: Have you ever thought about set design?
- **Speech Pathologist**: How about giving diction classes for singers?
- **Massage Therapist**: There is plenty of call for these on the road.
- **Chef**: Did you ever consider catering for touring bands?
- **Accountant**: Major touring attractions bring tour accountants on the road with them all of the time.

- **Financial Advisor**: In addition to the Artist Manager, a Business Manager is frequently employed to keep an artist's financial affairs in order.
- **Computer Programmer**: Build web pages for artists, or better yet, change the game forever a la Shawn Fanning, the creator of *Napster*.
- **Skilled Laborer**: Why not learn how to build a stage, or set up sound and lighting equipment? Few people get a closer look at what goes on behind the scenes at major concerts than the local crews that do manual labor.
- **Garbage Collector**: Research a company called Clean Vibes to see how two entrepreneurial young women built a business that takes them from major music festival to festival with a crew of music loving young adults that pick up trash in order to be a part of the experience.

The opportunity is there for those with the initiative, and the principles outlined in these pages apply. For those who possess the capacity to innovate—whether by doing conventional jobs differently or trying something new altogether—the possibilities are only limited by your imagination and your willingness to make the commitment. Please keep that in mind as we begin Section II: Building a Business Practically.

Create a Business Plan

Just because the career about which you dream happens to be in entertainment, this does not imply in any way, shape, or form that basic principles of business do not apply. It's called the *music business*, and it requires a serious commitment to both—the music and the business. Of course, the music itself is a given—no one need be reminded of that—but all too often artists forget (or ignore) the fact that establishing one's business requires equal attention, and to that end, I strongly advise creating a business plan.

The plan needn't be elaborate—at least not at first—nor does it need to be formatted in any "textbook" sort of way. As long as you document what you are trying to do, separating the art from the business so that you may chart the course of your development and the sale of your product, that is a satisfactory first step in the formation of a company (which is effectively what you will become).

Start by identifying who you are and what you represent. Note your sound and your style; to whom you compare yourself and why; how you fit into the landscape of the music industry as you know it; and what you believe makes you worth people's while.

Next, establish some basic goals and objectives—what you wish to achieve and how. Goals and objectives are essential to any business plan, even if you are having trouble identifying yourself. So, if need be, start here and worry about my prior suggestion later (as long as you address it in time). *Think globally, act locally* is a term you've probably heard before. You've got a big dream, perhaps a global vision in mind—but in order to make that dream a reality you'll have to start with what you know and build your business incrementally from there. Remember, before you sell ten million records you'll need to sell ten.

Yes, just ten—to people who are neither good friends nor family. Even that is an accomplishment, a small victory in itself, for anyone who is just getting going—much like ten thousand is to someone who is starting to catch their stride.

A conventional business in the twenty-first century builds its plan around four primary areas. They are:

- **Finance**: the development and management of a budget
- **Marketing**: product, place, promotion, price, and branding
- **Operations**: how your business will function and what it will need to do so
- **Information Technology**: Web presence, e-commerce, and related maintenance needs, as well as your computer hardware and software

All four fields have their place in the music business model as well.

Finance means, first and foremost, balancing your checkbook, paying your bills, and making fiscally responsible decisions when it comes to buying and selling everything from a van and trailer and auto and theft insurance, to rehearsal space, equipment, etc. Furthermore, it means accurate accounting of profits and losses on recording, touring, merchandising, and other items.

Marketing is the who, what, when, where, why, and how of presenting yourself and effectively increasing your sales both of product and at the box office. That means identifying the attributes and variables that make you who you are, and branding yourself accordingly (see "Brand Marketing," later in this section, for more).

Operations is the distribution of tasks (which is especially important without a proper music manager) and knowing what is required for implementation. Who balances the check book and writes all the bills? Who oversees maintenance of the van? Who works with the head of your street team to make sure the viral (or word of mouth—more on that later) marketing campaign is effectively building a buzz for the band?

Information Technology is exactly the same as stated above: all online and computer related resources. From Web maintenance, to antivirus software, to finding the next great resource for spreading the word about your music, there will always be a next great Internet technology—shouldn't someone dedicate time to researching where it will be and how you can use it to foster your growth and development?

All things large and small require attention to detail, as they don't just take care of themselves—and in my experience it's best that all members of a group be a part of the process and take responsibility for certain tasks. The alternative, when some take on more than others, breeds resentment over time and causes dissension within the band.

Now, in order to realize your goals and objectives in each of the above-mentioned areas, you will need to identify your assets and associates: what resources you have, or have access to, and who it is that you know—as well as whatever strategic alliances you may create. This list should include the other bands with whom you collaborate; the semipro videographer you know; your sister the graphic designer; even the friend in the gaming industry, who just happened to have co-created the Guitar Hero series, and with whom you brainstormed about a game based on the story of your band. These relationships will come in handy at some point in time. Organize them in some fashion which you can refer to as needed. Build your database of contacts both within the industry and without.

Once you've established your business plan, you may chart a course of action you can manage—one which follows a linear sequence and results in small measurable successes you can see. This will give you the confidence that you can do it on your own. Just be realistic and make sure your goals are reasonable. *Realistic expectations* is a term you'll hear over and again. Take your time, when you have to, in order to avoid skipping steps. Overnight success is unlikely, so you may as well do things right. Don't waste time—that won't help you—you'd only be cheating yourself. Be prepared for a long, slow ascent. As long as you're moving forward you will get wherever you are going.

The alternative to a plan is chaos, which only breeds frustration and disappointment, a lack of attention to detail, and worst of all, a false sense of hope. The music industry may be the business of entertainment, but it is a business nevertheless, and as such it requires a certain acumen. Don't ignore it—embrace it. Build your business one step at a time. Do it your way, if you wish—so long as you do it *intentionally*. Start at the beginning, write it down, track your steps, and see them through.

Commit To One Another

We were a band before we could play our instruments.

—Bono

Critical to the success of any joint venture is a commitment by the members to one another. I have worked with a number of bands that ultimately failed because one mate gave up on another, had a change of heart as to the direction of the group, or realized that what he had wished for wasn't what he thought it would be and threw in the towel as a result. That's why I advise being honest with each other at the time that the group decides to take things seriously; make sure you share a common vision and objective in taking your relationship to the next level—just as you would do with any other partnership, whether personal or professional.

There are good days and bad in every relationship, but when band members are on the same page, you just know it. You can feel that they have an energy which is both powerful and infectious. You can see that they share a chemistry which makes you want to foster their growth.

The same holds true for the commitment you make to a booking agent or manager, which is why I advise choosing your team very wisely. No one should have to walk around on egg shells, always concerned that his or her days are numbered. Nor should a relationship exist based on the perceived short-term benefit one foresees when aligning with another under questionable pretenses. Every decision should be discussed and agreed upon, but it should never be second-guessed with malicious intent. Every relationship should be a source of comfort for all, and all should know that the ups and the downs will be shared all around. When the relationship between band mates, or between band and manager, is strained, the dynamic can make for uncomfortable times—and unless you are one of Oasis' Gallagher brothers (or perhaps even if), that can very well spell trouble in the end.

I worked with one rock band I'll call Clouseau whose manager was unequivocally the best thing they had going for them. He was young and relatively inexperienced, but he was a voracious learner, with great instincts and only the best of intentions for his band. Unfortunately, one of the guys in the group grew pigheaded, thinking that things should be moving faster, and assumed the fault was that of the inexperienced manager; in fact, the truth was quite the contrary. In the end, they fired him, and he's gone on to do some great things, including running a successful label and managing another band that is doing well. Meanwhile, the group which he championed, who ultimately dumped him, broke up within a year of making their management change. Clearly, the manager was not the problem. The problem was that the commitment was one-sided. The band expected the world of him but wasn't willing (or able) to fulfill their end of the bargain. Once he was gone, their flaws were exposed, and with the writing on the wall, the band ran its course and was finished before they knew it.

All relationships run their course. Some end better than others. I cannot promise that a commitment to one another will necessarily hold a band together—only that it'll increase the chance of success and will teach you a few things along the way. One of the biggest disappointments of my career was the demise of another band that I'll call Sweet Lou. This Washington, DC-based group featured two guys up front: one on guitar, the other on harp. Their voices were fabulous, their harmonies beautiful. Their songs were catchy and their personalities were very appealing. They were great guys both on and offstage. They were tireless self promoters—they made fans everywhere they went, even if they weren't performing that night. They were the kind of guys who would be invited backstage to hang out on the bus of a band they had just met. People just wanted to be around them. Within six months of working together, they went from doing modest numbers in DC and a couple of other East Coast markets, to being invited to join major artists on tour, being offered a headlining slot at the great 9:30 Club, and garnering label and management interest from companies far and wide. Then one morning, just three days into a tour, one of the guys decided he wasn't "feeling it" anymore, and that was the end of that. Whether it just happened that way or the feelings had been festering for some time was never clear. His partner was obviously stunned by the news. As for me, that phone call was like a sucker punch to the gut—and a great learning experience once the pain subsided (months later). Sitting with music business attorney Alan Bergman not long thereafter, he told me, "That is why a band should always sign a contract." I consider that sound advice. It doesn't guarantee the band sticks together, but if a member resists, then the warning sign should be clear, and hopefully sparks conversation. Since that time, I have advised all artists with whom I do business to make that commitment and always be up front with one another, or recognize the writing on the wall and not be surprised when things fall apart.

The best bands ultimately thrive because they make the commitment. They lift each other up and make each other better. They work harder, knowing they've got others who see what they see and believe as they do. The cliché does hold true: the whole really is greater than the sum of its parts—but only when all participants are on the same page. A relationship in which one partner is more committed than another inevitably has problems, which all too often leads to disappointment in the end.

The DIY Approach

With all the technological advancements available today and an ever-increasing trend toward cost consciousness within the industry, one term that has become commonplace is what we call DIY. It's not a scientific discovery—in fact, it's nothing new—but the *Do It Yourself* approach is now an integral part of the development process. There are two reasons above all for this: first, it affords artists the possibility to sustain a career all on their own, by choice and not just necessity; and second, industry executives have no choice but to respect any artist who understands the process and can work within the system to establish a fan base that won't be denied.

DIY is what independent artists and aspiring professionals already do every day. It is what we have been talking about all along. Initially, it is what one does by necessity, when there is no good alternative. But as you acclimate yourself in the business, even just on a local level, things get tricky when the notion arises of passing your duties over to another. You are faced with your first test—your first real decision—when you, the artist, learn there are local agents you can contact who may be willing to book you at venues which you have had difficulty booking for yourself. Naturally, you figure, *Why not?* They have more contacts than you do, and you'll have more time to focus on your music, which is what you really want in any event. So you refocus your time on contacting agents rather than reaching the venues. But as reasonable as that sounds, I say, *Don't go that route*. Maintain your focus on doing the outreach yourself for as long as you can. It may sound like a better plan to develop your team sooner rather than later. For some it works, so to them all I ask is: please do your research. Be wary of the person willing to spend their time helping you, in spite of the fact that you don't make much money for them—which begs the question, what kind of business person are they to make this choice to work for a band that doesn't make any money? If you do choose to go down that road, take note of the venues into which they are booking you, and compare them to the venues other bands you respect are playing. Playing more often but in the wrong places with an agent handling your books isn't necessarily better than playing less but in the right venues and doing it on your own.

More importantly, I submit three notions to those faced with such a choice:

1) No one works harder for you than you;
2) The longer you do it on your own, the more you will learn about the business; and
3) The longer you hold out and make people want it, the more they will want to be a part of it in the end.

Certainly there are those who could handle your booking better than you could. The same goes for your marketing and publicity or your ability to get a profile in the paper or a song on the radio. Chances are you don't have the background and qualifications to effectively do those jobs. But then, you aren't expected to, and, chances are, if people aren't banging down your door to do so—not just one person, but several whose skill sets you are in a position to compare—then you aren't ready, and that is okay. What you lack in experience you make up for in passion. This means you will work harder than the next person will, for you are the only one responsible for your personal success. Why would you put your career in the hands of another? Furthermore, if the talent is there, then people will respect it—as will they respect your work ethic and interest in educating yourself—which will make them more inclined to help you and be a part of your growth.

So, instead of getting that agent or hiring that promotions company to run your campaign, I suggest holding out. Do it yourself by making good contacts and asking good questions, building incrementally every step along the way until your talent is undeniable and your knowledge of the business puts you in a position to understand the roles that you will ultimately outsource. This will help you make better choices when the time comes.

How do you do this? Beyond the hard work, it starts with little breaks. You make a strong connection with a promoter or the buyer for a venue, and you ask them for their publicity lists; then you solicit yourself to those people. You ask for suggestions about other places to play (whether in the same market or another nearby to your own), as well as other people you might talk to who could be willing to help. Repeat this process with all of your contacts as frequently as you can. Do it effectively, and it will pay dividends over time. Combine that with time well spent utilizing available resources: taking full advantage of the Internet to research networking opportunities, building friends and alliances/strategic partnerships, developing your brand, and moving your product.

Consider the number of independent managers who start their own labels (e.g., Silverback, Fueled By Ramen) or get their own distribution deals (e.g., Red Light, Everfine) rather than shopping their artists to the majors. They do so because they can, because a major label is no longer prerequisite to success, and because they already perform the duties of a label anyway (whether on their own or with the assistance of fellow independent companies that specialize in marketing, publicity, graphic design, radio, distribution, and/or retail sales). Rather than counting on another team to shepherd their artists' sales and allow influence over the direction of their careers, they are doing it DIY: managing the process themselves, in much the same way that I suggest young bands do.

Similarly, consider the man I believe to be the ultimate example of DIY—a man of uncompromising artistry and vision, who treats all elements of his career with the same respect as his music: Prince. A member of the Rock and Roll Hall of Fame since 2004, Prince is one of the most prolific artists of all time, a man who has earned the right to sit back and let others do everything for him. Yet he does exactly the opposite. Prince is the complete package: artist, multi-instrumentalist, personality, character, producer, manager, agent, and brand. He is a man so intent on controlling his own destiny that he deals directly with concert promoters to track ticket sales (adding additional shows in markets where sales are strong) and develops new kinds of promotions to tie to his concert ticket and album sales and build hype about upcoming appearances. Take for instance the 2004 Musicology Tour, where ticket holders were given copies of his new CD of the same name upon entry to the venue on the night of each show. Or better yet, even more recently, in 2007, leading up to an unprecedented twenty-one-night stand at the O2 Arena in London, Prince, ever mindful of doing things differently, cut an exclusive deal with London's *Mail on Sunday* to include copies of his latest release, *Planet Earth*, in every newspaper delivered. The result: millions of CDs were put directly into the hands of Londoners, and all twenty-one performances sold out. That's more than 350,000 tickets sold in just one market, grossing in excess of US$22 million!

Finding success in today's music business climate, perhaps in the current economic climate in general, is all about controlling your own destiny and not leaving it to others to make things happen for you. Prince perfectly exemplifies that fact, and his stick-to-itiveness makes him not just relevant but a visionary to this day. Going back to the basic premise that no one works harder for you than you, the DIY philosophy is all about establishing a long-lasting career by understanding the business and making it work for you. Best of all, due to the ever-increasing number of technological resources at your fingertips, the DIY approach is a more viable option now than ever before.

Identify Your Audience

There is a market for every style of music, so long as the quality is there. It's just a matter of knowing what it is that you do and accurately identifying your prospective fan base, then promoting yourself to them effectively.

Whether your music is straightforward pop rock, à la Nickelback or Daughtry, or more eclectic and/or avant-garde, such as cabaret rockers The Dresden Dolls, there are blogs, fan sites, newsletters, and various niche market-oriented zines on the Internet dedicated to all types of music. There are also live music venues, promoters, and festivals which cater to specific genres and/or demographics. Identify artists that are like you or yours, who share your style and/or sensibility, and are at your level or a step beyond. Find out where they play and to whom, how they promote themselves, and what makes them stand out. I'm not talking about superstars in whose image you fashion yourself—an emerging act from North Carolina who came together as a result of a mutual appreciation for U2 may learn a little something from studying their heroes, but not which venue in Asheville (for example) is most appropriate to break the market.

Once you've identified those artists who are like you, see how well their fans relate to what you do by posting on their discussion boards and passing out samplers at their shows. Consider this market research to determine whether you are truly a good fit. The more information you gather and the more people you reach, the more likely you will get the response you desire—even if you learn from the response that you have identified the wrong artists with whom to align and should be looking elsewhere for a more appropriate fit.

The same principles hold true in all areas of business. Just as you don't advertise the Super Bowl during *All My Children* and you don't market Huggies during *SportsCenter* on TV, you don't market a pop band on a blog dedicated to punk rock and you don't break a jam band passing out flyers at a hip-hop concert. Tapping into a community may take a long time, but once you have identified your audience and can market to them directly, you will save considerable time and money in the end, regardless of sound, style, or sensibility.

Hit the Streets

An effective grassroots campaign is the cornerstone of DIY. Building a buzz by word of mouth, whether literally, on the streets, or online is the fastest and most effective way to jumpstart one's career. If done well it's the most cost-effective means, too. No longer are traditional mediums like radio and newsprint a prerequisite to making one's name—and as more and more sources evolve (especially online) people are turning to *viral* marketing to target like-minded individuals more now than ever before.

Traditionally, street teams were literally people who assembled to hit the streets with posters and flyers, tapes, then CDs … spreading the music the old-fashioned way, one person at a time.

The advent of the Internet has changed the game for everyone. Now there are social networking sites, discussion boards and chat rooms, file sharing networks, and so forth—where people can go to find others who share their tastes and/or a platform to convert nonbelievers or just those who don't know. People can spread the word and the music to thousands at a time.

Of course, with so many avenues the market has become flooded with bands, which has ironically made it more difficult to get attention in spite of the resources available. Enthusiasts are bombarded with so much new music as they scour the Internet with extraordinary proficiency—the world literally at their fingertips—that they can barely keep up with the abundance of "tastemakers" on each scene who can identify the latest and greatest for them.

With so many places to post, not to mention the traditional means of flyering, it has become increasingly critical for an artist to mobilize and execute a viral marketing campaign with the help of a qualified street team that runs like a well-oiled machine. The team should consist of an active membership and an organized leader (or leaders) who can make assignments, watch for trends, keep an ear on the industry pulse, know where to go and what to do that will get the most attention to help foster the b(r)and, and build relationships and a resource center of their own.

Take Dispatch for example—the enigma of all enigmas: a band that built a thriving international community of fans who will travel thousands of miles for their band, despite the band never having signed with a record label and touring in a very modest, and limited, capacity. With a fan in Shawn Fanning, the founder of *Napster*, they had a natural advantage, some might say. Fanning made sure their music was all over the file sharing resource when it launched, flooding the market with their music and generating new interest by a means previously unheard of. But finding those resources is only half of the equation when implementing a successful grassroots effort. Motivating your team is of equal, or greater, importance, and this is where Dispatch excelled. After all, Dispatch fans weren't just energized—they were extremists to the core! Chad, Pete, and Brad knew that their good-time vibe and their regular-guy attitude made young people want to be around them. They realized that their fans wanted more than just to watch the performance—they wanted to feel like they were a part of the experience. So they encouraged them to show up early.

I remember the first time I booked a band at a prep school. It was a small school in Rhode Island. The band was the Princes of Babylon, a very talented live hip-hop group from Philadelphia which evolved as an off-shoot of G. Love's All Fellas Band. The school was small—if the entire student body had attended there still would not have been two hundred people in the house. But what was most memorable was not the performance itself but the enthusiasm of the students as they helped load the gear in and out of the venue. The PoB's manager, Jason Brown of Philadelphonic Management (G. Love & Special Sauce, Tristan Prettyman) and I joked for days after the fact that these kids' new favorite word was *monitor*.

"What's this for?"

"That's the monitor. It allows the band to hear themselves onstage."

"Hey, everybody, that's a monitor!"

"Cool, a monitor! Do you need help moving that monitor?"

"Are there any other monitors?"

"I want to move a monitor!"

These young people had no idea how to set up a PA. Nor did they know who the PoB were until that day. But we made them a part of the experience, and they loved it! They wanted to belong, to make a contribution, to be a small part of the process. Dispatch knew this too. They knew that something so simple as lugging gear in and out of a venue—the part of the gig that artists enjoy least!—would be fulfilling to their excitable young fans. So they indulged them. Who ever thought loading band gear in and out of a venue was a reward? Dispatch did, and their fans ate it up!

Playing into the hands of your fans by doing the little things has mutual benefit because fans want to feel like they know something others don't: that their favorite band is something special, and they were among the first to figure it out. Taking it one step further, in Dispatch's case, these fans weren't just the first to be in the know: they were actually a cog in the machine that helped to propel their favorite artist forward. And the satisfaction which accompanies such a relationship creates a love for, and loyalty to, one another that fosters a community which sustains and perpetuates itself.

That feeling of connectivity became a self-fulfilling prophecy for Dispatch, because they figured out that is what music is, what music *does*, for those who make the concert experience a part of their lives. Those moments where you feel a connection—that is what it's all about. From there, those young people with their savvy Internet skills (back before most of us knew what that meant) spread the word and encouraged others to make that connection through the music of their favorite artist. And that's *infectious*. That's how a viral marketing campaign thrives.

B(r)and Marketing

Commerce and art cannot function independently—
they must work together. That is the beauty of a
successful brand name.

—Donald Trump

I never took a class in marketing, but I learned a simple lesson about
the concept once that has always stuck with me: Marketing is finding or
creating a void in people's lives, then convincing them that you can fill
it. I'm sure there is a whole lot more to it than that, but it makes a lot of
sense to me in those simplistic terms. Whatever the product—whether
computers or clothing or toothpaste or music—a great marketing
campaign is always centered on building a brand name.

Take, for instance, Google. What better model exists for a global
takeover? Much like Xerox did years ago, Google has done something
few companies ever will—and I am not talking about consolidating
the Web, bringing the world to your fingertips with their simple search
function. What Google has so successfully done is to turn their name
(a proper noun) into a VERB! How do you find what you are looking
for on the Web? You don't do a query. You certainly don't Yahoo it.
You *Google* it, of course—even if you do your search on Yahoo! The
point is, Google keeps it simple. They focus on their strength—ease
of use!—even as they expand their capabilities. They are changing the
game because they do what they do better than anyone else, which
makes them indispensable, not to mention immediately identifiable.

Marketing a band is really no different. It's all about creating
an identity by marketing your product in a manner that makes you
immediately recognizable. People can then relate, understand, and—

more importantly—desire to own, use, and share. It is a concept that can be achieved by accurately identifying who you are and who you speak to (your target demographic), and shaping your promotional efforts to suit their wants and needs. Do these things well and you will ultimately build your fan base and increase your merchandising opportunities. In other words, *band* marketing is, in fact, *brand* marketing.

So how does a young band go about creating their brand? Perhaps it is their back story, if it sets them apart or gives people something to which they can relate. It might be their merchandise, if they can create a great logo; their look, if it is en vogue; something about their sound that captures their essence, whether it be their hooks or their rhymes, their blustering guitars or funky bass lines.

Consider Madonna in the early days: The Material Girl, as she identified herself and immediately became known; the Spice Girls, their names, and the products that followed; 50 Cent and the stories of his nine gunshot wounds; KISS and face paint. The very mention of their names or the brands they've created evoke images of the artists themselves, if not their songs in your head.

Beyond the superficial identifying characteristics, a band's live performance is another critical factor in creating a brand name and identity—how they engage their audience; how they work with one another on stage; whether they become known for being over the top with their antics and/or presentation; whether they focus on being polished and/or stylish in their own way. What an audience sees in or about a band, and what they come to expect when they attend successive shows—those characteristics which make them special, tangible or not—these techniques are equally important in building a brand. They will be further explored and examined throughout this book.

Of course, there is a flaw in my definition of marketing—an exception that defies the rule. Sometimes it's not about what makes an artist stand out. Sometimes it is the ability to capitalize on an existing trend and to build your base as a result. To a certain extent, this can be a valuable tool in creating a foundation, after which you distinguish yourself by highlighting what sets you apart. Drawing parallels between your own style and that of another helps attract an immediate audience. Therefore, if a young rock band bears a likeness to another that came first, then exploiting likeness to create an association will help them identify their fan base and draw people in. For example, John Mayer was often compared to Dave Matthews in his early years. Rather than distancing himself or denying the fact, he went so far as to impersonate his predecessor, thereby embracing the association, in a now-famous radio interview. (For the record, I do not apply any negative connotation to the word *exploit*, because by definition it simply means "to employ to the greatest possible advantage" according to *dictionary.com*. By this definition, shouldn't all marketing be exploitative?)

For further evidence, take a look at the *Billboard* music charts and see for yourself how much the industry has embraced the value of categorizing and associating like-minded acts. Where once there was a rock chart, there are now myriad charts for hard rock, modern rock, prog rock, active rock, indie rock, etc, etc. The logic seems to be that if a fan prefers one type of act over another, even within the same general category (i.e., rock), then they are more likely to look into similar artists who fall into the same specific category.

The industry benefits by targeting fans that share certain interests and/or sensibility, and as such are attracted to like-minded bands. Consider the Vans Warped Tour as perhaps the ultimate example. This longest-running touring festival features dozens of artists, big and small, on several different stages, allowing relatively new artists to perform alongside household names and exposing young acts to throngs of potential fans who already have an interest in the style of music they create. As such, the annual outing has become a natural breeding ground for the proliferation of future generations of like-minded artists and fans, which in turn makes the success of each annual tour a self-fulfilling prophecy. That, in essence, is the brand the Vans Warped Tour has created.

There comes a point at which a band must also highlight what makes them stand out by establishing their own identity. If they do not, they reduce the possibility of building a fan base that will support them through thick and thin, buy their records and attend their shows over the long haul, when their hits (if they have any) dry up. Or worse, a comparative study between airplay, album sales, and concert attendance may reveal some interesting results: there are a handful of artists who have released numerous top-twenty hits yet fail to sell a comparable number of tickets when they take their craft on the road. The problem is, there are some artists who write hit-making records, with songs that connect and fit in the landscape of their respective genre—and from which they make a very good living from recording and publishing royalties—yet, for whatever reason, they fail to establish a brand name, and ultimately they become another nameless, faceless number in the crowd. When the airplay slows down, so too will their careers, for the association between artist and music was never made.

Consider Grammy Award-winners Train, who have sold millions of albums worldwide and had three top-twenty hits on the *Billboard* Hot 100 charts; Five for Fighting, whose hit "Superman (It's Not Easy)" became the unofficial theme song for hope in America following the horrific events of 9/11; or Blessid Union of Souls, who had six hit singles between 1995 and 1999, including "I Believe," which reached number eight on the *Billboard* Hot 100. Can you picture these bands in your mind? Do the names Pat Monahan, John Ondrasik, and Eliot Sloan mean anything to you? They should, given their hit songwriting abilities. But they probably don't. For whatever reason, their respective brand names never truly caught on; they are nameless, faceless bands who never established an identity in the landscape of popular music.

On the other hand, consider Coldplay. Here is a band that achieved critical mass in the United States in the year 2000, when "Yellow" reached the tipping point. At first they were identified as another UK rock band cut from the same cloth as U2 and Travis—an association worthy of attention. But soon they outgrew the likeness. Perhaps it is the longing in Chris Martin's voice that people find wanting in their lives; the hope in those lyrics, or the soundscape their music creates, is distinctly their own. Perhaps it is the band's social activism, or Chris Martin's marriage to actress Gwyneth Paltrow, which heightened the band's own celebrity as a result (though the band did not become known for either of these things until after they crossed over into mainstream music culture). Or perhaps it is the combination of all of the above which makes them stand out.

Whatever the reason for their success, the Coldplay brand has become ingrained in the hearts and minds of people around the world. They are unique and immediately identifiable. When you hear their songs you know the band, and when you hear the band (or see their name) the songs will ring in your ears. That is brand marketing at its finest.

Making Friends/ Building Relationships

The music business is a relationship business. The significance of making personal connections cannot be emphasized enough. It is imperative to cultivate a community of associates—with fellow artists, with fans, and with industry professionals alike—at every stage of development, especially in the early days. Therefore, taking full advantage of as many relationship-building opportunities as possible is essential to having a lasting career.

As with all personal relationships, the little things are what matter most. They are what separate the good from the great. An exchange with an avid fan at an event may not seem so important at the time, but the impact of such a simple interaction is immeasurable, as it can lead to the creation of a fan for life. Every conversation can be a catalyst to a lasting relationship. A strong first impression can transform an average fan into a valuable member of your team, channeling his enthusiasm for your band into a chain reaction amongst his peers.

Similarly, when dealing with fellow artists and professionals you want to make every exchange count. For a touring band, no matter what the size of the venues you play or the number of heads in the house, the chance to befriend the other bands on your bill is not to be undervalued. Building friendships with other acts can lead to trades in each other's best markets as well as touring opportunities down the road. Bands from the Boston area may know this concept as *the bro-down*. It's a term often associated with the Mighty Mighty Bosstones who have credited bro-ing down with their rise to prominence and contribution to the ska revival in the 1990s.

Taking what MMB did for ska to the next level, consider the four-and five-band tour packages that have become the norm in the indie and active rock scenes. With one or two bona fide headliners, plus two or three emerging artists (who are typically either labelmates or friends) on every bill, tour stops are transformed from simple concerts into exciting events. These packages have become a microcosm of touring festivals like the Warped Tour, Lollapalooza, and OzzFest—each of which has become a phenomenon in its own right by breaking new bands and paving the way for entirely new genres to garner mainstream attention. But even before you get to that level, it's important to treat every opportunity like it's a big one, taking nothing you do for granted. When booking a date at a local club, keep in mind that a slot on a stage is not just a show—it's a business decision that makes you a part of something that is costing someone money. Your opportunity is a result of someone's investment, and it's your responsibility to make the investor look good.

Talk to talent buyers about what you need to do to promote your gig. Ask their advice. You'll be surprised at how quickly they respond and give you more opportunities down the road, because they will recognize your interest in the process and will genuinely appreciate your effort.

Beyond the gigs and the fans, it is also important to ask people's opinions and respect what they have to say. If you are given a business card, follow up without hesitation. Heed the advice of those who have come before you; listen more, talk a little less; and keep buyers, labels, managers, and agents aware of your activities. These are the types of things which show other people that you "get it," and in time they will lead to good things.

Strong support affords a promising future and the possibility to achieve longevity. A radio-hit single can take an artist to the top, but it doesn't guarantee him or her a future. Building a foundation, one fan at a time, will ensure a lasting career. Consider O.A.R. or Guster, for instance: these are acts with no massive radio success and no platinum-selling records to speak of. Yet they have forged a bond with their fans that cannot be overlooked. They have created a sense of community that makes fans feel a part of something significant. They continue to grow via grassroots means, making use of emerging Internet technologies to maintain a sense of awareness of what they are up to on and off tour.

As a result, they will always have a home at a label and an agent who keeps them on the road for as long as they want to play.

The same principles apply to aspiring music industry professionals who spend their day knee-deep in the trenches. They learn quickly that the talent they represent is only half of the equation, that it takes certain savvy to open doors, and that visibility is a major factor. Making people aware of what's going on, smiling and dialing to stay on top of your business, and using e-mail to keep people in the loop are vital factors in drawing attention to your artist(s). Concerts, festivals, and industry events are essential vehicles for generating face time and cultivating your own exposure to peers. Recognition garners respect, generating support within the industry that leads from one introduction to the next.

It may seem like a daunting task at first to enter an industry filled with unknowns. You don't always know what leads you where and who leads you to whom. But, in time, you'll find that the business is quite small, and your ability to connect the dots will help you realize that the degrees of separation between you and industry movers and shakers are closer than you think.

The best of the best get where they are because they stay ahead of the relationship curve. They keep their eyes open and hand on the pulse, always pursuing new leads and never letting an opportunity pass them by. It's a lesson I learned a long time ago, reinforcing the importance of the relationship building process in an indirect sort of way. I was a young agent, inquiring about avails for a then-relatively unknown rapper named Kanye West. I called Cara Lewis at the William Morris Agency, who is among the elite agents in the world. She knew where I was calling from, but she didn't know me—probably had never heard my name before and could easily have passed on my call. But she didn't. Cara was engaging and kind, in a no-nonsense/get to the point kind of way. I asked my question and she answered, so I thanked her for her time. Then she said something I'll never forget. "No need to thank me," she responded in kind. "I'll always take your call. You're money."

It was a gratifying response, which has stuck with me to this day. She needn't have bothered, could have easily passed me off on one of her assistants. But she didn't. Instead, she engaged me and treated me like I wasn't a waste of her time.

I have always tried to follow Cara's lead. I make myself available as often as I can and hope others will do the same for me. A casual exchange may or may not lead somewhere, but the possibility takes just a moment either way. As the industry continues to expand and evolve into the twenty-first century, so too must we all, taking full advantage of every opportunity to foster new acquaintances. For in a business built upon relationships, there is always room for another.

Teamwork (and Team Building)

First and foremost, if you are in a band: Coming together with your mates and getting everyone on the same page, working together with common cause, is the single most important thing you can do in the early years—and having a built-in support network will put you well ahead of the solo artists out there. Recognizing each other's strengths and weaknesses, appreciating each other for what you bring to the table, trusting each other—yet maintaining some checks and balances to keep each other grounded in reality—all of these attributes will make a significant difference in the long run, and should be taken seriously, and to the limit, before you look for outside support.

Simply stated: If you know what you've got and are motivated to achieve, then why put your career in the hands of another? Why risk the possibility that someone else might not work as hard for you as you would for yourself? The best of the best, no matter what their discipline—whether artist, agent, manager, or other stakeholder—take it to their own personal limit first before enlisting the support of an outsider. Though you may think you are ready for the support, be truthful with yourself about whether you really are ready and whether you really need the assistance, or if you just don't care to do the job yourself so would sooner pass it off on another.

That said, in time you will find there are people soliciting you—not just your friends and your family, who want to lend a hand—but fans and even local industry types. When this happens, the first instinct is often to turn over the reins, hand them your books, put them in charge of the street team, let them act as manager—who cares—anything that alleviates pressure and takes some of the work off your plate!

Of course you think to yourself, *No. I wouldn't do that. I wouldn't jump into something so important without forethought.* Oh no? Perhaps not. Perhaps you would take your time and thoroughly assess your situation—to make sure you are doing what's best. But I assure you, the pressure is great when you've been slaving away—committing more time than you ever dreamed, time you feel should be spent writing and rehearsing, getting back to what made you choose this path in the first place. I don't pass judgment on those whose first instincts are to jump headfirst into what appears to be a good thing on the surface—not if they've been deeply entrenched in the business for months, if not years, and are starting to question whether they'll ever see the light. However, that does not mean I suggest you take the leap.

Find the time to do your research on everyone you meet. Look beyond your obvious greatness and all the reasons to sign a blank check—which is effectively what you are doing when you turn your career over to someone else—and ask yourself some serious questions. For instance,

- Why are they interested in you?
- What is their motivation?
- Are they passionate?
- Do they believe in your music?
- Is it all about money?
- Can they make you any money, or do they just want a piece of yours?
- What is their background?
- Do they have a proven track record?
- Do they have a reputation, good or bad?
- How would this relationship reflect on you?
- Can you trust them?
- Can you work with them?
- What would be the nature of the relationship?
- Beyond what would be their role, how would you interact?
- Do they want to be your partner, your boss, or your friend?
- Which of those roles do you seek in such a person?
- Do they have a plan?

- Do they have specific goals and ideas?
- Are they open to your ideas too?
- Will they help you achieve your goals?
- Are they more concerned with their own goals than yours?
- Can you be successful together?

Keep in mind that you are building a business, and, while friends are great, what you need are associates. You need people with whom you can be open and honest, trade ideas and information, and—of equal importance—people you feel comfortable having represent you. I'm not just referring to your agent or manager. Each and every member of your team, no matter how significant their role, shares in the responsibility of shaping a first impression of you that most people "get." Think about that. What they say, and to whom, and how the association reflects, will shape preconceived notions before prospective fans ever hear you, see you, and/or meet you—if any of those things ever do occur. That means, in a nutshell, that if you work with one agent, even on a nonexclusive basis, then you may never get consideration from another. If you allow just anyone to join your viral marketing team—even just one person who happens to rub others the wrong way—then you may lose out on earning appreciation from any number of future concertgoers, who may never give you a chance.

Sound crazy? I once represented a pop rock band that had a street team coordinator who, in a strange twist, had a way about her that apparently turned potential fans off—two of whom happened to be friends of mine. These two were young women whom I frequently ran into at shows all over town. One night I told them about this band I represented and they informed me they had no interest, that they were aware of the band but believed them to be obnoxious and arrogant and couldn't care less about the music they made. As it turned out, their impression derived directly from their observations of the way the street team coordinator spoke to others on various message boards which they monitored. Fortunately, I convinced these young ladies to give the band a chance. Soon thereafter they began bringing their own friends to the shows, and, as a result, the band's fan base continued to swell. But if not for one particular chance encounter, these young friends of mine might never have taken interest in the band—all on account of one individual who had no real stake in the band.

The same basic principles are true of aspiring professionals too—whether agent, manager, promoter, producer, label owner, or other player. The acts with whom you associate reflect on you in many ways—especially with respect to your knowledge of the big picture and your taste. So, ask yourself the same questions as above.

I don't mean to suggest that all questions have answers—certain situations require a leap of faith. But all situations deserve thorough analysis resulting in conclusions with which you can live. I'd like to say that people won't judge you based on the company you keep, but, I assure you, they will. So, if you aspire to work with elite industry professionals, ask yourself whether you can justify your choices. Expect that they will ask themselves the above questions too, anytime an opportunity to expand their team presents itself, as you should want them to do. Commonality in the answers to those questions is the only way a team will work well together.

Internships

Whether you are an artist or an aspiring professional wishing to work for an existing company or start one of your own, an internship is a tremendous opportunity to gain practical experience, make personal contacts, and get a better overall understanding of the business. How does one go about getting an internship? Once hired, how does one make the most of the opportunity? What constitutes a successful experience most likely to result in a job? These are the questions I am asked most frequently.

With countless young people lining up for a peek at what goes on behind the smoke and mirrors, it goes without saying that paid internships in entertainment are few and far between. Yet, that doesn't stop the resumes from flowing in to all companies that announce they are looking for help. That's why I believe the best way to position yourself for hire is to build a resume with volunteer experience. Whether it's a local or campus radio station, a student paper or regional magazine, an activities group at your church or school, an area festival or concert series—the opportunities abound. To those who are motivated and willing to keep their expectations low, the experience can prove invaluable and reflect well to prospective employers.

There is a school of thought that believes that when writing your resume you should use a certain amount of overstatement in order to drive home your exceptional skills and abilities. I, for one, disagree with this method and believe it has no place in the music industry. Excessive use of power words like "impeccable," "exceptional," "extraordinary," and the like are more of a turn-off than a turn-on. Those who highlight their supervisory skills and fail to exemplify their ability to work as team players do little to impress. While a resume most definitely should illustrate all of these qualities—leadership ability, self-confidence, good communication skills, and the like—candidates should temper both their words and their postures to reflect equal ability to take direction and to be a part of a team. That balance reflects an understanding of the politics and the culture which exist in the music industry, and is the reason some highly experienced candidates get passed over in favor of those who have done less but display a willingness to learn more.

Once in the door, to make the most of an opportunity given, as a good intern you must learn quickly how to make your presence felt without getting in the way. Make positive contributions at the appropriate times without being overeager. Bring absolutely zero ego to the table, check prior knowledge at the door, and commit to trying something another way—even when you think you know better. Possessing enough background to follow direction, but not so much experience to mistakenly convince yourself you know more than they do, is a highly desirable quality. Prospective employers want to know that you will do what you are asked in the manner that you are told, without worrying that you might think you know a better way and disrupt the flow of business as a result. Let me put it differently: Don't ever assume.

Additionally, I find the best way to avoid any disruption to the routine of the company for which you intern is by taking the initiative to develop a weekly update/progress report, even if it isn't requested. Include what work you have done, what you have learned from the experience, what questions you have, what goals you have made, and how you think you might like to achieve them. By keeping such a log you are forced to think about the work you are doing and put it into perspective, which in time will help you to understand the big picture. In the process, it will provide your employer with a frame of reference which will help with your learning curve and can guide you through your experience in a manner which will allow your goals and objectives to be realized. Such a log is the key to what I call The Three Os: maximizing Output, Organization, and Opportunity. This is not to say you should not ask questions. You should never stop asking questions, no matter how far up the corporate ladder you climb. Even when you know the answer, it's good to get a different perspective every now and again.

There is a certain catch-22 in the music business—on the one hand it is up to the individual to take the ball and run, but on the other it is imperative that you make zero assumptions and do things only as specifically instructed. That means it is the responsibility of you, the newcomer, to assess the situation, acclimate yourself quickly, ask good questions, then take the direction given, showing the utmost respect at all times, and develop an efficiency model that ensures that the job gets done and progress is effectively communicated—all the while recognizing that it takes a very long time to earn the respect and trust of the team you are hoping to join. Detailing your progress and helping others to manage you will foster those relationships, enhance your value, and allow your superiors to develop a track that can work for everyone.

All that said, there is one caveat about which I must be clear. Please do not look for an internship with the intention of building a relationship on behalf of a band you know or with whom you already do business. This is a piece of advice that was specifically instructed to me at my very first interview with the company where I first interned (Rykodisc USA). They told me that if I was there with the hope of getting a band I knew signed then I should leave and never return. They explained that my function was to learn by working for them and understanding the reasons for working with the artists they would choose. I have reiterated this sentiment to every intern I have interviewed since. Yet, twice in my years it became evident within days that a new hire had lied and was clearly angling for just that—and it was little surprise that these two individuals were my worst interns ever, who not only failed me but failed themselves in the process. They were always angling when they should have been absorbing information— and in time they ultimately lost my favor, as did the bands with whom they worked.

There will come a time to leave a mark and carve your own niche— once you've earned the opportunity. Understanding the methodology of those who came before you will help you get to that point. Seek out those people who will take you under their wing, and ask yourself, *Why do they do what they do?* In time, a successful internship should help you answer that question and allow you the opportunity to do as well for yourself, if not better.

Politics, Politics, Politics—and the Conscious Decision to Take the Long Road

As with virtually all things in life, there are politics which dictate the way things get done in the music industry. There's no governing body or oversight committee and nothing set in stone (though at times you wish it would be)—just some basic, unwritten rules and regulations which can serve as your guide, or an obstacle, depending on the approach that you choose. Respecting those that have come before you, appreciating those that offer assistance, not biting the hand(s) that feed you—these are just a few of the tenets which, over time, will establish your course and reputation.

Knowing who is connected to whom, and how you get from A to B, is all part of the political game. Think about your career like any government official running a campaign: you generate support and awareness by establishing a name for yourself. Then you leverage your contacts as you move through the ranks, using the platform you are given and the latitude it permits to spin your message and advance your cause.

The best thing that can happen to an aspiring politician, or young artist or industry pro, is to be recognized by someone who is higher on the food chain and who is willing to throw you a bone. This person might open a door or make an introduction to an associate, offer you an appearance slot or merely point you in the right direction. Practical advice is a valuable commodity in an industry that often seems guarded like a well-kept secret.

Whether you benefit from such an instance or simply see things in a different light, you might consider going out of your way to say thank you. Even if there is no immediate gain from the information provided—should it go nowhere at all despite painstaking efforts— you might show gratitude nevertheless. Such an association may be a small victory in and of itself, and the appreciation you show—and the character you display—may lead to far greater triumphs in time.

As previously discussed, the music business is a relationship business, and the way you treat those relationships can make or break your career. Conversations should always be calculated. How you speak to people, the deference you show, and what you do or do not say are all very important. Proper respect results in reciprocation. Going the extra mile for those who do right by you is imperative. Overlooking an opportunity, no matter how seemingly inconsequential, should be done with great caution.

Learning when to do what is a big part of the game. It's a distinction which comes with awareness, of who and where you are, what you are trying to do, and with whom—and failure to appreciate the potential significance of every situation is what I call the conscious decision to take the long road. Say, for instance, that you are offered the opening slot on a great show, but unfortunately you cannot commit. Some might say, oh well, and casually move on to the next, believing similar opportunities will inevitably come along. But the wise young professional remembers the gesture, and shows gratitude down the road. Perhaps you do a favor in turn, even though the original favor never came to be. Maybe you simply prolong the conversation, by checking in from time to time in order to keep the lines of communication open and stay on that person's radar, in hopes that another such possibility will come along. The person who takes advantage of the situation, whatever it may be, will more than likely be rewarded for his or her efforts in time.

Of course, things are not always so cut and dry. Politics become complicated as an artist moves up through the ranks, and ambiguous situations present themselves. For instance, what do you do when a national touring act comes to your town and asks you to open for them at a venue you might otherwise headline on your own? You face a dilemma—what should you do? Does it diminish your reputation if you support another act in such a venue, or does the association with the other act serve to heighten your exposure and thereby benefit you over time? From a political stance, this can be a tough call—balancing local versus national politics. You'll want to weigh all the options and handle the situation with care. You should try to determine why you've been asked, and what you could realistically gain—whether this is an opportunity to build a relationship and/or leverage one slot for another with the act or the presenter. On the other hand, it is possible the show needs you more than you need it—and your participation is only good for everyone else. These things happen, and there are times when saying thanks, but no thanks is the right call—but failure to recognize the politics involved and act accordingly is, again, a conscious decision to take the long road.

Another sticky situation that may one day arise, should you be so fortunate as to gain the favor of multiple promoters in a market, is when offers start coming from more than one and you face the decision of which will benefit you more, both in the short term and the long. Maybe one promoter helps to establish you in a market, then another comes along saying he can take you further in the end. Perhaps the former is better at providing opening slots, but the latter has the reputation for booking the headline acts with whom you want to become associated. Sometimes one choice propels you further ahead, opening you up to a larger audience and exposing you to new fans—both within the industry and among prospective concertgoers who gravitate to one promoter more than another, or prefer one venue more than the next. But what if both paths lead to the same place? Sometimes the choice is clear, but sometimes it's not so clear. That's when the politics get interesting. Balancing loyalty with reputation, commitment with playing the field, and knowing if/when to change directions mid-stream can be a very sensitive situation. The same goes for deciding when to switch from one agent to another, or with which label you should sign.

Politics determine so many things in our lives. Therefore, thoroughly vetting each opportunity presented and projecting the potential ramifications is always worth the time. Why waste months, even years, making uneducated choices and letting opportunities pass you by? Understand the political repercussions of your actions, and make the conscious decision to take the shortest path from Point A to Point B.

Walk a Mile in their Shoes

Ever wonder what the person on the other end of the phone looks like—who they are, where they work, what their lives are really like? It's a common misconception that the music business is one big party—that beneath the glitz and glamour, the sex and drugs are just a part of life. Some people think we wake up in the afternoon thinking about the show that night, saunter in to the office whenever, have cocktails with lunch, more cocktails before dinner, then hit the show—fashionably late, of course—to party like a rock star until the early morning hours, at which time the afterparty begins. There's an aura of cool that surrounds the industry, and even those who get a taste often have trouble seeing past the fun and games. But the reality is not quite so sensational, alluring as it may seem.

For an agent, a manager or label executive, a publicist, promoter, or marketing director, the day usually starts early, sometimes around 7:00 or 8:00 AM, and ends sometime between 6:00 and 10:00 PM, depending on the day. Of course, that's in addition to a show, if there happens to be one that night. Ask anybody who maintains an active roster of artists and you'll find that most work between fifty and seventy hours per week—at a desk, on the phone, writing e-mails, building relationships, doing research, strategizing, making plans—trying to stay ahead of the curve, with their ears to the ground and their noses to the grindstone. That's not just to become a revolutionary—that's just how they make a living. It's not unlike anyone else.

Of course, they listen to music for much of the day and they talk about that which most consider extracurricular activity. But they are not necessarily looking and listening for the same things as the "average person." For them, music is their job—and in the end there are going to be those days when they feel as though they are processing TPS reports.

Talent buyers, tour managers, and venue employees have it a little differently from the average industry professional—especially those who work with small independent venues and keep an office in the concert facilities themselves. Consider this: for hours each evening, seven nights a week, large quantities of alcohol flow. Have you ever hosted a party—not a swanky affair with wine and cheese, but a bender in your college apartment? You wake up the next morning, walk down the stairs, and the smell makes you want to vomit (again). Sound familiar? Well, imagine your office is a cramped little closet that opens into the living room.

Now imagine that you sit in that office takings calls from ninety-seven artists and agents a day—all of whom want something from you, many of whom are convinced that they are the next coming of Jesus Christ (without any concept of what that means), and very few of whom possess an appreciation of what is expected should they be so fortunate as to play your venue. Still think these folks are living the dream?

Some of them just might be—they are doing what they love and loving what they do, and in spite of the way it might seem, most are more than happy to take the time to get to know you, if you'll just try to understand them, too. But understanding that they don't owe you something, and that it's up to you to make yourself stand out—these are among the first lessons that you need to learn. With neither greatness nor a proven draw to speak of, you mean little to them early in your career. But your courteous and respectful nature and your interest in understanding the way they do business can lead to a personal relationship that will keep you in their minds, should an appropriate situation arise. Once they determine you are worth the investment, a relationship may ensue.

You may say that ingratiating yourself to these people is all well and good if you can get them on the phone—but sometimes that is the hard part. So, are there any short cuts which expedite the process rather than being hit or miss? Many of the answers to this question are covered later on in the book—suggestions on proper presentation, solicitation dos and don'ts, and the very next entry on, "Living in the Gray." But for sake of this specific chapter on walking a mile in their shoes, I suggest that you consider just one more piece of advice that can help you along the way: learn the routines of the people you attempt to reach. If their office hours are from 12:00 to 2:00 PM , but you don't know that, and you call between 4:00 and 6:00 PM daily—well, you may never actually get a live person on the phone. Rather than beating your head against the wall, if you find that you never reach someone at a particular time, make a note and try other times until you connect. When you do, ask questions: When is the best time to reach you? Do you keep specific hours? Do you check email more often than you are available by phone?

Understanding their routine will help structure your own—and while your politely inquisitive approach earns you respect, you will also learn how to save time (not to mention your sanity). Moreover, walking a mile in their shoes will help shape your perspective—giving you a peek into the big picture, one professional at a time, by seeing the way others go about their business—and formulate a way of your own.

Living in the Gray

There is a very fine line between persistence and stalking. It is a gray area, where persistence is prerequisite; over-persistence is hard to define; and stalking is, well, illegal. It is an area which cannot be fully explained, as it comes down to the slightest of margins. There is an episode of the Seinfeld show in which Jerry attempts to explain the difference between first and last place in a horse race won by a nose. He explains it this way. First place: head forward, neck extended out. Second place: head and neck straight up and down. Last place: head tilted, neck back. That margin, often the result of a last-second surge, may be the smallest, most incremental difference, and yet it is the area in which an aspiring music industry professional must live, for as long as it takes to succeed, because walking that line and knowing when to surge are critical elements when breaking into the music business.

So where do you begin? As mentioned in the previous chapter, doing your research and learning the routines of the people you solicit will help you in two ways. First, it will help you schedule your own time more effectively. *That cannot be emphasized enough.* There is no sense beating your head against the wall because every time you call someone—at whatever time is convenient for you—you can't seem to get them on the phone. It is better to find out what hours they keep and what times they are most likely to be available. Second, it will help you in establishing your rapport, allow you to ask them how frequently checking in will make sense, and give you the opportunity (in time) to press that limit, in order to get from them what you seek. "Stalk me gently," is the advice a talent buyer once gave me, and I couldn't illustrate the point better myself. These people are aware of what you go through; they know what's required to reach them and have an impact.

They expect you'll press the limit; they'll recommend it in some cases, knowing fully how to crack their own shell. So you must stay one step ahead, if you can—and not just for you, but for them. Allow me to repeat that: you must stay ahead, if you can—and not just for you, *but for them*.

Adding to the level of difficulty, of course, is the fact that the gray area varies from person to person, as everyone has their own routine, their own tolerance for diligence, for pushiness, doggedness, determination, and resolution. These are all characteristics with which you will—make that *must* (if you aren't already)—become familiar, and soon.

There is a point, however, where a line can be crossed, and with some people that constitutes the point of no return. If, for instance, the instruction is, "Do not call me for a couple of weeks," I find no fault with a call ten or twelve days later. If that first call happens to go unreturned, a follow-up a few days after that is okay. But to begin the pursuit within the first week, or to make several calls in a day, shows a clear lack of understanding and disrespect to the solicited person, and it may prompt a succinct, "Please lose my number." And that will be the end of that.

Similarly, it is never okay to show up at someone's door unannounced, whether it is to drop off a package, ask a random question, or anything else; nor should you call someone's home uninvited. I can appreciate the perspective that a face-to-face discourse allows for a greater opportunity to really get to know someone. But when you are soliciting someone's attention, an uninvited visit is not the appropriate way. I can't emphasize enough how far that crosses the line.

On the other hand, bumping into someone at a show, at a conference, or a festival—whether calculated or otherwise—is a far more acceptable option and is something one might conveniently *make* happen with a little forethought. People who frequent the venues they seek to perform in should have little difficulty finding opportunities to network and make themselves known. Visibility is a persuasive tool, and passively selling yourself just by being around is not without merit.

Of course, it's a little more difficult to make yourself visible at a venue two hundred miles away. So if you can't, or don't, frequent a venue, consider asking a leading question every now and again to see if you can't make a chance encounter happen on your own. For instance, if you happen to be visiting Rochester, New York, and know the Water Street Music Hall has a big show that night—something you can find out by checking their calendar online—you might say, "I suppose you'll be at the Maceo Parker show?" And if they say yes, you might say, "Me too—perhaps I'll see you there." *Create the opportunity.* Similarly, if you will be attending a festival or industry conference, do some digging to find out who will be there—then call them, and find a way to ask them the question, "Will you be there? Perhaps we can connect?"

Making things happen means putting in the time to develop a keen sense about people by thinking on your feet. It requires asking the pointed questions, reading the signs, and understanding what is and is not being said. It takes confidence and a level of comfort to know—not guess, mind you, but really *know* (and appreciate) the fine line between persistence and stalking. And that is living in the gray.

Practice Humility

Too many artists enter the business thinking that what makes them unique is what will make them successful. In theory, this may be true. However, there is a certain level of knowledge and perspective that must be realized first, and that begins with the understanding that the universe does not revolve around you just yet.

My all-time favorite expression, which brings a smile to my face every time, is: "I don't know if you've heard, but I'm kind of a big deal."

It sounds so incredibly obnoxious one might assume it's a joke each time they hear such a story told. Believe me, the first few times, I assumed the storyteller was exaggerating, or that they were simply retelling an urban myth. That is, until the first time I actually heard it said to me. Oh yes, and I've heard it more than once!

A certain amount of narcissism is tolerated in the entertainment business, perhaps because it takes so much self-confidence to make a living performing live (though there are innumerable examples to the contrary: Dave Matthews, Tracy Chapman, Cat Power to name a few). But the notion that *artists* (say it with me in that museum-snob tone) have a penchant for arrogance is all the more reason why it's better to be humble.

Humility is always appreciated by the many nameless, faceless people working behind the scenes. They may be facility employees, journalists of some sort, or college student-activities types who do it all, from soup to nuts, for the emerging artists that come to their campus. There are few things worse than getting big-timed by an artist, however talented he or she may be.

People who deal with musicians on a regular basis care less about what happens on stage than they do about the way they are treated. In other words, a great show can be spoiled by an intolerable ass. The performance is a given; that's why they come into contact with you in the first place. Don't expect them to put you on a pedestal just because.

Don't overlook the reality that for a band just getting started, a kind word from a green room wait staffer just might be the difference-maker that earns a return trip. And if you are a band on the rise, don't be fooled into believing you are better than the journalist conducting your interview, no matter what you know or feel about their show, column, blog, or even high-school student paper.

Even the big ticket sellers get more favorable treatment when they are unassuming and show respect and appreciation to those who make it possible for them to thrive. Self-confidence is great, but narcissism should be kept to oneself. Practice humility and watch your opportunities increase, along with the size of venues you will play, the quality of the bands you will play with, and the number of units you will sell.

Creating Nontraditional Performance Opportunities

Recognizing the difficulty of breaking into a new market where an act has neither a draw nor a buzz, sometimes it's worth taking nontraditional performance opportunities into consideration to lay a foundation. Playing at colleges and universities, prep schools, and high schools is always a great way to start, as these offer a decent payday and a manageable, targeted community base to which you can promote yourselves. Further, if you ask the right questions and/or do your research there is the possibility of garnering press and getting spins on the campus radio station—two things which are not readily available to most emerging artists. Unfortunately, school shows are neither easily attainable nor appropriate for many acts whose music skews to a different demographic. Further, there isn't always a direct correlation between a campus gig and "the scene" you seek to be a part of at a venue in the same town—even when they are just blocks apart. Therefore, sometimes the best thing to do is to create a new scene all your own.

House parties are one way to get something going—whether it's at your own home, that of a friend, in the barn of a local farm, or perhaps at the inn of a faraway fan who would happily play host to your show. Think of it much like any other party that you might play, except instead of you being there to entertain at the party, the party would be specifically thrown for you. As at a public venue, attendees would pay a nominal fee to attend, with the money going to pay for the artist and expenses.

Renting a hall, a church basement, or an available multipurpose space is another approach that can produce great results, especially when targeting an underage demographic that can't get into the nightclubs and bars. In fact, a growing number of professional promoters do shows in such venues—and why not? If you know there is a market for live music and have the ability to bring it to the people at a place already familiar to them, then it sounds like a no-brainer. Say, for instance, that a local youth center has dozens of kids who would happily pay five dollars to see a show on Saturday afternoons—why not start a concert series featuring quality touring talent? Everyone has to start somewhere, and who knows what possibilities it may lead to in time for the bands, the fans, and the promoters themselves?

Consider the bands Apollo Sunshine and State Radio. What these bands did to foster their buzz, with the help of a student label called Heavy Rotation Records (formed on the campus of the Berklee College of Music in Boston), was go into various small towns across the Northeast that otherwise don't get much great music close to home. They found out what spaces were available to play and where the underage kids would be willing to go—the ones who didn't necessarily have a car. Then they booked the performances on a percentage basis, brought in their own sound and lights, and hired popular local bands to open the shows. The local bands would then distribute flyers, hang posters, and promote the events at all the area hot spots where students in those communities would go, knowing it looked good for them to be opening for an emerging national band. Thus, much of the work was done for State Radio and Apollo, and the kids invariably came to the shows. And while the bands didn't make an overwhelming amount of money, the number of CDs they sold was unbelievable, as the kids were too young to be wasting their money in bars. They gladly paid ten dollars to commemorate the time that they heard the next great band play a few short miles away from their suburban homes, where their parents would gladly let them go.

The nontraditional performance route doesn't work for everyone. But the truly committed artist will try just about anything to build a base. The benefits are well worth the time, as the odds of bringing an audience to see you in a traditional venue will increase and be appreciated by the person who gives you the opportunity—not to mention that there is also the ability to improve the quality of your performance before appearing somewhere industry professionals might see you, thereby positioning yourself for greater success over time.

To Tour or Not to Tour

Artists are always quick to assume that touring early on is the only way to succeed, and there are several seemingly reasonable arguments in favor of this. It makes the band tighter the more they perform, gets their name out in markets where they otherwise wouldn't be, puts them in front of an audience that otherwise wouldn't see them play, and creates the impression that they are on the up-and-up. It's also a source of pride and a feeling that they are "doing something," as opposed to standing still. But for every sound argument in favor of touring, there are equally sound counterpoints worth noting. For instance, while touring can make a good band grow tighter, it can also expose avoidable flaws to an audience who may take a less-than-favorable first impression away from their experience. What's worse, without a buzz in anticipation of a performance, the odds of a good crowd attending in the first place are significantly less than they would be if said artist decided to wait. Finally, performing to a small crowd night after night has a demoralizing effect on one's psyche.

I believe it's better to create the impression that a band is on the rise by focusing on the few performances they play, in the most well-thought-out, targeted venues in the region where they reside. Furthermore, I suggest going all out promotionally each time a band performs, thereby increasing the chances that the audience will grow, which will prove the most compelling evidence that a band is "doing something" that anyone could possibly seek.

Start in your backyard, and build your base there. If you are from Chicago, then set your sights on your immediate surroundings, and don't sweat your first New York City show. Create an event out of each performance, employing the best marketing initiative that zero dollars (or as close to it) can buy, pulling out all the stops that you have learned, and making sure your street team enacts the most effective viral brand marketing campaign you now know how to create. For those truly exceptional nights (such as CD-release parties), reach out to area press, telling them what makes this date special.

In the early months and years you'll want to play your backyard frequently, trying to make a name for yourself as fast as you can. Then slowly you will scale back, from weekly to monthly, then every two, then every three—making your audience want you more and more, thereby increasing your draw over time.

Subsequently, you should start to identify those markets in the surrounding areas that make sense for your band to thrive. For instance, a Boston band with a college appeal may want to start in Portsmouth, New Hampshire, and Burlington, Vermont, and spread outward into Syracuse and Rochester, New York, plus New York City and Philadelphia. On the other hand, a Boston band with a blue-collar appeal might instead target Hartford, Connecticut, and Portland, Maine, then Providence, Rhode Island.

Of course, there are also select venues in seemingly unlikely places where niche audiences seek niche bands that otherwise don't seem to fit within the context of the area—which is all the more reason to do your research prior to booking each gig.

So, then, how do you identify the right places to play? Start by finding out where bands you consider similar to your own will perform and book a show there. Then, be honest with yourself about the audience reaction, and don't hesitate to ask the venue's talent buyer afterward if he or she believes the room is a good fit for your band, and vice versa. The answer might be no. Don't be afraid of that possibility, however desperate you might be to find places to play. It's better to know you are not in the right room, and/or do not have the support of the buyer you solicit, than to beat your head against the wall trying to book another gig because that's better than facing the reality of your situation. Over time, you will gain confidence in who you are and what your band represents, and it will become obvious to you which venues you can grow and which are worth leaving behind.

When you have identified the right places to play, and the buzz begins to increase, give careful consideration to the number of performances you can do without overloading yourself, and be mindful of the amount of lead time you require to properly promote them, with the objective being to turn each one into an exciting event and not just another show. Furthermore, consider that limiting said performance dates to weekend nights in the early stages of development generally increases the odds that casual fans will attend.

When you are finally ready to start building outward, consider adding one new market per trek, so you aren't breaking too many new places at once. If you are lucky, and promote yourselves well, the buzz will start to precede your arrival. When that happens, you will know it's time to start adding more new markets with every new run, and over time a long weekend will become two full weeks, then three, then six, and so forth.

Touring is an inevitability, to some degree, for most artists. After all, unless an artist has a string of commercial hit records, developing a touring base is the only way to sustain a lasting career. But it's not something to rush into simply because it sounds like the thing to do. Want to try it, every so often, just to see what it's all about? By all means, do. There is a lot to be learned on the road—some good, some bad, and some ugly. Not every band can handle it—no matter how advanced they are—so finding out sooner rather than later may be well advised. Nevertheless, I personally have learned to oppose touring for the sake of it. I have been a part of several ill-conceived touring plans in my day, as have most industry professionals when they first cut their teeth. The tendency to get out there and do it while you are young is overwhelming at first. It's a lesson most artists learn the hard way—which is why I fault no one for failure to heed my warning. But in time they learn the value of building their backyard so they may always have something to come home to after making their next foray into the unknown.

Play the Game, Don't Play the Game but At Least Understand It

> In business, every business, the bottom line is understanding the process. If you don't understand the process, you'll never reap the rewards of the process … Part of the process is doing your homework. You have to know what you are getting into first.
>
> —Donald Trump

Many artists consider the business side of making music to be burdensome and go out of their way to avoid getting caught up in it. Some believe it taints the process, others simply don't care. Some become successful in spite of their refusal to play along, but most struggle for their entire lives and never realize their dreams—not because they can't but because they don't know how. Some of that is born out of ignorance—a specific lack of knowledge that keeps them from seeing the light—and some of that is born of stubbornness—from a personal place, deep inside. So many artists have the potential but refuse to listen to those who can help.

The former problem can be easily overcome. The latter takes time and patience. We write that off as artists being artists—anyone who knows "the type" can relate. Unfortunately, however, there is a third type of artist who is not so easily helped—the artist who outright refuses to play the game, believing that he or she is above it. Recall Terrence, from "Everything Takes Longer than You Think." A very spiritual guy—his father was a preacher—he was so caught up in denouncing conventional wisdom that while he acknowledged the existence of the game, he refused to believe that he had to play along. It was as though he lived in a parallel universe in which things would work out simply because that was his will. At times, I wondered if perhaps he was right. After his first of two nights supporting Wyclef Jean, Clef asked him to sit in with the band. After the second, Clef suggested he finish out the tour. Unfortunately, Terrence expected the game would always come to him, but that was not the case. He did a few dates with G. Love and the crowd reaction was great, but he burned his bridge when he failed to appreciate his role as the opening act. He showed up with different backup bands with a different instrumentation each night; rolled into the venues at his leisure on the final night just ten minutes before he was scheduled to go onstage (with a six-piece backup band in tow); and blamed everyone else for the "miscommunication." I had hoped the relationship with G. Love would evolve into something greater as a result of these dates; called in a favor to make them happen. Needless to say, my relationship with Terrence soured soon after.

Of course, art is art and typically outlives its creator, so my intention is not to write off their creation. Many of the great composers and painters of the last several centuries have not lived to see their legacies evolve into something far greater than that which they experienced while alive. The quality of their work and the context in which they create it is not for me to judge. However, for those with an interest in success during their lifetime, my message is this:

> Play the game or don't play the game—it doesn't matter to me. The industry doesn't need more talent. There is tons of untapped potential in the music world yet to be discovered. All I ask is that if you wish deep down inside to be successful, rather than railing against the machine you might first try to understand it.

Whatever your artistic means of expression, to be successful you must first recognize that there is a world around you which is accustomed to looking at things a certain way. You need not conform but you should have an appreciation for protocol and understand they won't conform to you either—at least, not just because you say to. You've got to get people's attention and earn their respect first—and the best way to do that is to show them that you understand their point of view before you dismiss or attempt to reshape it.

The great Neil Young once expressed his feelings on songwriting as follows:

> I look at writing songs as like hunting for a wild animal, but you're not trying to kill it. You're trying to communicate with it, to coax it out of its lair. You don't go over and set a fire and try to force it from its lair, or try to scare it out. When it comes out, you don't want it to be scared of you. You have to be part of what it sees as it's looking around, what it takes as natural, so that it doesn't regard you as a threat. To me, songs are a living thing. It's not hunting to capture. I just want to get a glimpse of it so I can record it.[1]

Mr. Young was referring to his process: the way songs come to him. But I think this quote says so much more—not just about a method for writing, but about a method of connecting with what's inside of you and understanding how it relates so that you may effectively communicate it to the world. Simply put, when a person introduces himself, he doesn't do so by clubbing someone over the head. He doesn't scream, "This is me, motherfucker. Like it or not, I don't care!" That is, not if he's trying to make friends. He may convey that sentiment over time; that's his prerogative, and, if so, he may be respected for it or embraced by a certain subculture. But initially, when, say, you are the new kid in town, it's often better to be a part of what people see as they look around and accepted as someone who belongs.

Deep down inside, I believe that's how radio programmers subconsciously think. I believe the same is true of people working for record labels when they are signing a new artist. They want the songs to be taken as natural, as though they belong within the context of

---

1   Wilkinson, Alec. "The Open Man," *Rolling Stone Magazine*, 26 January 2006, RS 992.

their surroundings. That's how you sell records or fit within a format, even when you are doing something different. It's just another form of relationship that must be established—in this instance within the context of music itself.

Even if the songs are intended to protest the world in which we live, as with punk bands like the Ramones, the Sex Pistols, and The Clash, or political bands like Public Enemy and Rage Against the Machine—even when the intent is to lash out, alarm, and cause strife—the method must appear natural, and true. It must fit within a context to which people can relate.

In the book *Bumping into Geniuses*, author/industry veteran Danny Goldberg talks about how Nirvana, the ultimate anti-corporate rock band, understood the game that they played. He describes how the band knew from day one that they wanted to be successful, and in spite of the way they would come to be remembered, they went great lengths to be relevant to the mainstream music-loving public, even in spite of themselves at times. He details Kurt's hesitation to appear on the cover of *Rolling Stone* magazine but explains that ultimately Kurt understood the positive affect a cover photo would have. So Kurt did it, but on his own terms, wearing a shirt that read, "Corporate rock magazines still suck."[2] An iconic, yet equally ironic, cover indeed.

Neil Young says songs are a living thing—I say they represent them, too. What's more, I say understanding the ways of the industry is not unlike understanding his songwriting process. So, whether a song tells a story, represents a feeling, or recollects a moment in time, in order to communicate that sentiment and fit it within the context of the musical, as well as the corporate, landscape, you must find a way to engage people first. In other words, by understanding the game that we play you earn the respect that gets you attention. Only when you have that may you fully appreciate the voice you've been given and use it to teach the world something new.

---

2   Danny Goldberg, *Bumping into Geniuses* (New York: Gotham Books, 2008), 200.

Simultaneously Preparing for a Life after Your Performance Days Are Done

If you are familiar with the world of college athletics, then you have more than likely seen numerous interviews with coaches who talk about preparing their players for life after sports. They do so because they know full well that even the best Division I programs produce very few successful professional athletes with lasting careers. Coaches at the professional level do the same; they profess the value of a college degree, the importance of investing wisely, and the reality that all good things come to an end. These same principles apply to the music business.

So many young bands form while musicians are in high school and college, and so many elect to bypass getting their degrees in favor of giving their music a shot. I don't have any problem with this in theory—though I advise keeping open the option of returning to school later and being mindful of the fact that a lasting career is unrealistic for most, so it's better to shed the blinders early on.

To increase the chances of having a career in the music industry, though not necessarily on the stage, a number of artists recognize the possibilities that exist for former musicians who immerse themselves in the business and learn their way around from the inside out. This is yet another reason I suggest educating oneself about the various facets of the game.

Perhaps you handle the books while playing the bass in your band and take accounting classes on the side. Should things not work out on the stage, you might follow another career path doing tour accounting or business management. Perhaps you do the advance work or the bookings—in time, doors may open for you to become an agent or a tour manager.

The possibility of parlaying experience in one area of the business to making a move in another is common in the music industry. Agents become talent buyers, talent buyers become managers, managers become label executives, and musicians become any and all of the above—and so much more. Each of these possibilities are interchangeable, as cross-pollination within the industry runs rampant.

Knowing what you are getting into as a musician and learning your way around the industry helps to prepare you for your life after your performing days are done and increases the odds that you can somehow earn a living in the industry you love. Even if you don't stay in the business, you'll gain valuable experience that may translate to other industries and give your résumé a little something extra that other job candidates will not have. Of course, fulfilling your requirements to get that degree may be worth consideration as well.

Section III

Presentation Put Simply

Press Kit: Proper Presentation

Whether you are the lead guitarist in an active rock band or do public relations for a public company, your press kit serves more or less the same purpose, and therefore it should contain the same basic elements. It is your introduction to the world and the public persona you wish to convey. It's the foot in the door to venues, agents, managers, promoters, labels, publicists, and everyone else worthy of solicitation. It should be clear and concise, representative of your character, and, simply stated, it should encapsulate your essence in as few words as possible.

There are bands that use gimmicks or create visuals that stand out: color schemes, glossy paper, vinyl folders, and the like. There are bands that keep it simple and let their music speak for itself, using plain white paper void of spirit or personality. Then there are those bands that understand the happy medium, where the aesthetic value is inherent, and the presentation allows the viewer to get a sense of the artist in easily digestible bites, compelling them to explore further.

Many industry professionals say that an unsolicited package is lucky to get thirty seconds of someone's time. In my experience, this is more or less true. I peruse the press kit, pop in the music, and look for a compelling reason to delve deeper—to get some sense of the artist's potential both visually and audibly, through the words and images on the pages as well as in the music coming through the speakers.

That said, there are things that draw me in and things that cause distraction, and it's a very fine line between the two. Folders quickly get tossed, bright colors get overlooked, and dense text with no punch gives me pause. I, like so many, seek immediate gratification. I don't need to be bowled over in mere seconds flat (though that certainly is my preference), but I also don't have the time or the patience to navigate through fluff. I'd rather be told that you are a new band from Wichita and are committed to earning your stripes than read through churched-up ramblings (as if I won't discover the truth) because you believe your skills in deception are tantamount with those of a Jedi knight.

A good press kit is more like a portfolio—a sampling of your best work, organized in a manner that puts your best foot forward. If you are truly creative as an artist, and your kit captures a style all its own—then you are an exception, and in that case I take note. Perhaps your kit is round like your disc or in the form of a small book—à la the CD sleeve to Damien Rice's brilliant *O*. But that's rarely the case, so, in general, I say, save the generic folders from the supermarket and spare me the superfluous crap. Stop trying too hard; keep things as simple as you can. Slap your logo across the top, consider a splash of color (but not too much), make use of **bold text** and *italics* to emphasize your points, and save the dollar and a quarter per package on the needless distracting junk—over time it will add up (especially when you factor in the savings on postage)—and reinvest your savings in other facets of your business.

So now you know what a press kit should and should not be, and it's on to what should be contained therein. In brief:

1) **A one sheet**: your bio, summed up in as few words as possible, using buzz words and phrases, hinting at the story you have to tell;

2) **A quote sheet**: the best of what has been said, by the best sources available;*

3) **A short list of career highlights**: appearances and accolades, radio stations spinning your songs, television placements, and the like;

4) **A press photo**: see the next chapter for suggestions; and finally

5) **A CD** (LP, EP, or sampler): recognizing that the listener may not give the music much time, so choosing the first couple of tracks carefully is of paramount importance.

* With respect to press clips and quotes, it's important to gather all press, and a master kit is the place to store them. But for general solicitation purposes, it's better to include catch words and phrases from well-known publications. The impact of a significant source is greater than a multitude of local zines when soliciting someone's attention.

That said, if the person being solicited is based in North Carolina, then a mention by the Charlotte Observer is worth noting. If the person being solicited is from a college or university, quotes from other campus papers will get attention. Therefore, knowing your reviewer and his or her perspective can be a difference maker—so flexibility and forethought are worth consideration.

Contact information should also be included on every piece of the kit, just so it's always at hand.

If the story sounds interesting, the sources are worth note, the photo makes some statement, and the CD is worthwhile, then doors will open. It's really as simple as that.

Of course, as I write I do realize that the growing trend in the music industry—in all industries for that matter—is to move forward using technological advancements. And to that end, electronic press kits (EPK) are an increasingly viable means of solicitation and should be developed in much the same way. Creative license is more tempting, as the possibilities are endless if you have the graphic design skills. Nevertheless, the essence must remain clear, as the same principles do apply. Simplicity, simplicity, simplicity. If your art is pure, then let it speak for itself and use your skills to enhance, not disguise.

Finally, always put the correct name, with the correct spelling, on all cover letters. You wouldn't believe how frequently that gets fouled up. There is no better way to lose someone's favor than by addressing them incorrectly. It shows a lack of consideration and a deficient attention to detail. Similarly, spell check is a function in all word processing programs (that I know of), so why not make it an automatic option every time you create a new document? Would you release a CD with glaring wrong notes? Of course not! So why would you do so with your press kit?

Album Photos and 8 x 10s

There's really just one simple rule when having your band photos taken—whether with instruments or without, on stage or in the street. Whatever the circumstances, regardless of the vision, the key to a classic group shot is this: *Look like a band.* I don't mean a caricature of a band, with your lead guitarist looking like Slash, a bottle of Jack in his grip— just something more than a random gathering of nondescript people whose connection to one another is unclear.

Whether you prefer to resemble a band of brothers or a band of idiots is entirely up to the discretion of you, the artist (or sometimes the photographer, depending on his/her vision). The photo may be stylized, or it could be understated. It might say a thousand words, or perhaps just a few. Sometimes photos capture a moment in time. Sometimes they capture an essence. They needn't be overthought, and they don't have to scream rock 'n' roll; they just have to say *something.*

Yet, all too often what gets selected for printing comes off looking like a random collection of miscellaneous people, awkwardly forced into a picture together—which is both irresponsible and wholly unnecessary. It's not as though I'm suggesting a group hug, and it doesn't necessarily matter that a band look alike.

Check out the cover of the Beatles' *Abbey Road.* Four men, dressed in their own unique way. John is in a white suit and matching shoes, hands in his pockets. Ringo is dressed to the nines. Paul is in bare feet, cigarette in hand. And George is in denim from head to toe. They walk in stride, though Paul is out of step. They stand alone, but are clearly connected. It's a completely casual shot, and yet it says so very much about them all in the end. They are (were) a band, despite their individuality. That photo exemplifies my meaning, despite a lack of evidence in the picture that they even play music at all.

Be a band. Be a unit. Have fun, or don't. Be yourselves, whoever that is. Select the photos that make a statement, in the same way you select your songs.

Creative Ways of Thinking about the Basics

The chapters on brand marketing and creating a business plan touched on the importance of finding and marketing an identity by exploiting those characteristics which make an artist who he or she is. But on a much more rudimentary level, there are certain things an artist can do to garner attention, not by looking deep within but by thinking differently about the basics.

Consider that a certain amount of rebellion has always been implicit in rock 'n' roll. We can all conjure images in our minds of artists who stand out visually, for one reason or another. Trends like grunge make you think of flannel, glam makes you think of big hair and makeup, emo evokes images of skinny black jeans and tight vintage tees. So why not take this "rebellious" approach and apply it to your marketing campaigns, your stage presentation, and your online presence?

For instance, on a very simplistic level, when everybody else is making a rectangular poster, why not make yours round, or diamond shaped? And if everybody else is making flyers in the same basic colors, why not make yours bold? A little imagination can go along way. Create a logo that draws attention to you—or encourage your fans to create one for you. Spice things up a little bit to make you stand out.

Similarly, when crafting your stage show—not just your song selection or the clothes that you wear, but the overall aesthetic you wish to create—ask yourself what you could do to visually enhance your appearance and compliment your music to provide your fans with a heightened sensory experience. Would ambient lighting add to the overall entertainment value of your show? What about projecting images onto a screen? The things you can do with a laptop computer and a projector are remarkable and not overwhelmingly expensive. Of course, on an even more basic level, a banner with your band's name and logo (and possibly your Web URL) on it would at least remind casual observers of your name.

Given the things you can do with a computer, an aspiring artist in this day and age is well advised to monitor the ever-increasing number of technological advancements that allow artists to reach fans online in new and different ways. From *MySpace* to *YouTube* to *Facebook* and the like—knowing what the new technologies are and staying ahead of the curve allows you to be a part of the revolution and not just a slave to the trend. But beyond the performance and the marketing materials, the most basic way to make a new fan is to figure out how to touch someone's life on a personal level. So ask yourself: how can I make an impression, not just onstage but off, without reinventing the wheel? How can I make that connection without ever really changing my routine?

I recall a promotion I did with Gavin DeGraw when he was first coming up. We booked him to headline a charitable event to benefit two music foundations, one of which ran a songwriting competition in conjunction. The premise of the competition was to encourage young people to create a presentation explaining what the song, "I Don't Wanna Be," means to them personally, with the winner to receive a free concert.

The submissions were both random and extremely diverse. The top two were an essay on existentialism and a video presentation of a group of schoolchildren singing along to the chorus and speaking over the verses about who they were and what they wanted to be when they grew up.

What made the promotion so simple, but so special at the same time, was that all Gavin had to do was show up somewhere and play his piano for forty-five minutes on an afternoon which conveniently fit into his tour schedule. Yet the impression on the people who contributed to this project, and especially on the individuals who won the free show, had far greater, more long-lasting implications. First they had to internalize the song and really think about what it meant to them, thereby establishing a connection. Then, in the case of the winners, they had to come together and make this video with their classmates, which their teacher said was a wildly enjoyable experience for all of them. And finally, they got a once-in-a-lifetime experience—an up-close and personal, free, private concert. All of this adds up to a strong probability that these children made a series of memories for life, and all Gavin, his manager, and I had to do was participate in (and in my case, produce) a charitable concert event.

Apply the creative juices that you otherwise reserve for your music to the business approach that you take. Don't worry about reinventing the wheel; just take advantage of the resources available and the interesting opportunities which present themselves. Make yourself stand out from the rest so that you increase the number of prospective fans who may take a closer look and see what you are all about. If done effectively, it becomes a self-fulfilling prophesy. Make yourself stand out if you wish to be a standout. Creativity abounds.

Performance Techniques, in Brief: Humanizing the Experience

As previously addressed, staying true to yourself is extremely important in making a positive impression on stage. Yet, equally important in maintaining this expression of "truth" is the ability to humanize yourself by showing different sides of your personality visually as well as audibly. Rock icon Bruce Springsteen once said, "To be lasting, you have to look at your audience and see yourself, and they have to look at you and see themselves." You have to be genuine, authentic, and show more than one dimension. Therefore, consider switching it up on stage, breaking free of conventional ways. Show you are more than just a performer standing in front of a mic, strumming a guitar, or pounding on the drums. Establishing yourself as a human being above all—superhuman though your powers may be—is critical in building a fan base.

A singer is not "emo"(tional) all of the time, standing solemnly behind the mic wearing his heart on his sleeve. A "punk" is not always angry, thrashing about every which way. Many drummers aspire to be front men (and women). Many singers like to pound on the drums now and again. Why resist the urge? For whom are you filling a singular, predefined character role?

A front person should not stand behind the mic all day long where X marks the spot at the downstage center position, strumming a rhythm guitar and singing as if standing before a plate glass window, void of any connection to the people all around. The same holds true for a guitarist or a bass player, even a keys man or a drummer. One needn't be defined by a constricting amount of space.

Many singers wear guitars around their necks, not to play but to hide behind. They might think that their rhythm guitar parts are critical, but often they are just subconsciously justifying the action because it sounds better than admitting the simple truth of the matter: they do not know how to move comfortably about the stage, nor do they know what else to do with their hands. That is not to undermine rhythm guitar parts in general. Sometimes they are vital to the music. But sometimes it just might be better to take the instrument off and move about, grab the mic with your hands, and reach out to your fans standing before you.

A great way to connect with an audience, whatever size, is to move with them, dance with them, exchange ideas and energy. Seize the moment! Why stand on a spot predetermined to be yours? Why fall back on conventional ways? You are not the Beatles on the *Ed Sullivan Show*. Chances are your fans have been to a show before—whether to see you or somebody else. You don't have to be OK Go on a treadmill— just consider doing your thing a little bit differently from everyone who's come before you. You might consider doing it in a way that gives your audience a sense that they know what you are all about.

If you like to move, then move. Even if you don't, you might try it anyway every once in a while. You don't have to dance like Justin Timberlake. If you like to trade instruments, then trade instruments. It was part of Dispatch's charm. Be versatile. Show people what you've got. Harmonize. Connect. Be free. Be everything you are, and all that you aspire to become!

If a song paints a picture, then a concert is an exhibition. Don't paint one picture over and again—show different sides of your personality: different moods, different tempi, different colors, different styles. Switch it up—not for show, but to show who *you* are. Make your audience see that you are a lot like them, and they are a lot like you. I do not prescribe doing too much, nor overdoing at any time—being a caricature of a front man is not the solution. Unless you are David Lee Roth, don't behave like he does. But being comfortable with who you are and conveying your personality on stage makes you "real," and that is something worth note.

When Less Is More: On Stage and on Record

> Sometimes a few well-chosen notes are more powerful than a barrage of impenetrable sound.
>
> —Ben Hughes, *Esquire Magazine*, on Ben Ratliff's *Coltrane: The Story of a Sound*

> Get in, get on with it, get it over with, and get out.
>
> —from the movie *The Court Jester*

There is a tendency in art, as in life, to overindulge and overdo, typically for the sake of self rather than others. In music that can be especially dangerous, which is why it is advisable for all young artists to understand the concept of *less is more*, and when and where that applies in the recording process, in songwriting, and in performance.

Self-indulgence is something all people struggle with now and again. It's a tendency that needs to be tempered, to be controlled as best one can—especially during the introductory phase, when it's better to ingratiate oneself slowly. Consider the dating process. When you go on a first date, is it really a wise choice to dominate the conversation with exaggerated personal stories that tell your date too much? Do you come on strong to make them aware that you REALLY WANT THEM BAD, or do you play it cool? If desperation is what works—and there are artists for whom it does—then I say, go with that. But, generally speaking, I submit that it's better to leave your companion wanting more and agreeing to see you again than to give away too much too soon and run the risk of damaging the relationship before it begins.

It's the same in making music. When introducing yourself to the world, or even just the twelve people sitting around the coffee shop, it's better to casually engage. Show great taste in selecting from your repertoire wisely and great restraint for giving just enough *but not too much*—rather than hitting them over the head with everything you've got and giving them more than they can handle. *This is not to say you shouldn't put everything into your show—only that you should be selective with the material you choose.*

Choosing your material wisely is especially important in support slots when an audience doesn't know you. "Hit 'em hard and go home," they say. A short set that is carefully crafted to exemplify the best of what an artist does is more likely to leave people captivated and interested in hearing you again. On the other hand, a set which drags on for too long can cause listeners to become uneasy, keep an eye on their watches, or go to the bathroom or the bar.

Similarly, when releasing a debut record, especially an independent soft release (one that is made public without pomp and circumstance as opposed to a major campaign), it is often better to select the best five or six cuts rather than to put every song you ever recorded onto the first disc out the door. An EP should give listeners the taste they desire and leave them wanting the full-length LP when the time is right.

Let's face it—few artists have the repertoire to release a full-length record with nary a weak track when they are just getting started. Heck, most great artists in the twilight of their careers run the very same risk every time. Isn't it better to put your best foot forward by releasing only the best of what you've got, rather than giving away too much with throwaway cuts for filler?

Of course, many artists think of their songs as their children—they don't necessarily know which are great and which are not. They think of them all being equal. They see characteristics which appeal to them, dramatic effects poetically achieved, or subtle riffs which ring true in their minds—whether they connect with others or not. But regardless, even when an audience is engaged, it is better to leave them hanging than to satiate them completely. Consider most television series as a comparison. At the end of each episode, and especially the end of each season, there are situations which get resolved but cliffhangers which force viewers to tune in next time. You want your audience to wonder what's next. You want them to talk about you, think about you, and desire you. You want a second date, and a third, and a fourth. The more involved you become, the more intimate and engaging your conversations will be—and it is then that you begin to share more of your music, when you've got them feeling your vibe, hanging on your words, and listening for the nuance in your voice.

The *less is more* principle applies to the songwriting process too, where subtlety and restraint allow people to hear what's between the lines, to feel what the artist feels, and to give in to the hooks and melodies which tell whatever story you wish to convey. Listen to U2's "One," and you'll understand what that means. The song is simple. There is no need for clutter, exaggeration, or overemphasis.

Of course, there are times when you want more, so the rule is not absolute. As an artist's career evolves, longer shows, double discs, and box sets become a way of giving back—a way to indulge your fans when they want it most. That too is the case with friends and lovers, when it is appropriate to share all of yourself, to let it all hang out because they love you no matter what. When that time comes, then *more* becomes more. But until that day—consider *less*.

Practice Does Not Make Perfect

My high-school tennis coach, Mr. Murch, taught me an invaluable life lesson when I was about fifteen years old. He said, "Practice doesn't make perfect. *Perfect* practice makes perfect." To me, these are words to live by.

In context, what Mr. Murch was telling me was that it didn't matter how many balls I hit, or how many backhands and forehands I took every day. If I wasn't hitting the ball the right way, if I changed my grip and developed a bad habit, then I was ultimately doing more harm than good, no matter how much time I spent on the courts. This is true in every facet of life.

As a musician, you can play for hours at a time but if you aren't properly warming up and down, or you develop a habit of squeezing your throat and straining to reach the high notes, you can really do damage to your career.

As a band, if you spend hours during rehearsals running through songs but don't really work through the tough parts—whether it's the intros or bridges or the segues between songs—then you'll never be as tight as you can be (or perhaps as you think you are), and you aren't as likely to make it big.

The same is true for those aspiring to work in the music business and band-related activities. For example, some years ago I was the booking agent for a pop band that I really thought was on the verge. Unfortunately, however, their approach to doing business always drove me crazy, because the bandleader was extremely headstrong and he always had to do things his way. He couldn't take criticism at all—

anything remotely negative drove him into childish fits and it took its toll on the band. He would tell me that the band spent hours each day working in their makeshift studio/office, yet in two years' time I saw little progress. Their draw was inconsistent. Their performances were, too. They had a street team that they insisted was amazing. They worked hard and loved what they were doing (both important qualities) and had all the makings of a successful organization, except one—they weren't doing the right things. They weren't flyering the right shows; they weren't building relationships with the right fans; they weren't sending the right message to the millions of CD buyers and showgoers within their reach. As a result, they didn't go anywhere, which ultimately forced me to walk away.

The point is, you may have the talent, the songs, and the will—but without the understanding of how to do the job you severely diminish the opportunity to succeed because practice doesn't make perfect, and being proactive doesn't necessarily produce results. Doing the right things is the only way to achieve, no matter how much time is spent at your desk, onstage, or in the field, or how great everyone feels about their organization.

So, seek out opportunities to learn more about the business. Find mentors and ask their advice. Perfect practice is the only way to make perfect. To me, that's a lesson for life.

Solicitation Dos and Don'ts

Do: show respect to the person you solicit, whatever the purpose for your outreach initiative

Don't: be arrogant, obnoxious, or rude (even when you aren't getting the attention or responses you believe you deserve)

Do: be creative

Don't: be so *over the top* as to distract the reader/listener from your stated purpose

Do: know what you are talking about and who you are talking to

Don't: waste people's time

Do: represent yourself in the best possible light, highlighting what specifically it is about you that should make them want to learn more

Don't: specifically state that you are someone they should want to learn more about

Do: represent yourself in a manner which tells people why a relationship *could* be mutually beneficial

Don't: tell them right off the bat how you are going to help their business, or that your relationship *would* be mutually beneficial

Do: pursue them aggressively

Don't: behave in an aggressive manner

Do: spell-check everything, especially people's names! ·
Don't: address people incorrectly, whether by misspelling a name or getting it wrong altogether (it's truly amazing how often this happens)

Do: seek opportunities to meet them face to face (conferences, festivals, concerts, etc.)
Don't: show up at their doors unannounced, regardless of your intentions

Do: listen to their instructions/requirements for solicitation
Don't: ignore their instructions/requirements for solicitation (side note: this one would seem to be the most obvious of all, but, inexplicably, it might be the least)

Do: be honest
Don't: lie

Do: offer points of reference
Don't: name drop to excess

Do: impress
Don't: impose

Do: be specific
Don't: be vague

Do: figure out what makes you unique and convey that to the best of your abilities
Don't: expect people to understand what makes you so special and/or think they will treat you unlike anyone else

Do: send materials upon request
Don't: send large unsolicited files via e-mail

Do: be clear that you intend to follow through on solicitations, whether via phone, e-mail, or snail mail
Don't: send an e-mail saying, "If you want to work with me then let me know," and leave it at that as if you've done your part

Do: pursue any and all leads possible
Don't: discard a lead because you think it is a waste of time

Do: take all suggestions into consideration
Don't: assume you know better

Do: take all suggestions with a grain of salt
Don't: take anything too personally

Do: know when to move on
Don't: give up

How to Advance a Performance

A common, but easily correctable, oversight is undervaluing the importance of properly advancing your performances. Sometimes an artist simply believes they are prepared, which would seem to render additional conversation redundant. Sometimes it's a result of ignorance—it's possible that they just don't know any better. Sometimes it's the simple fact that dealing with the whole "business side" of the process can feel like a burden instead of an opportunity to an artist, and, as a result, some just don't care. But the fact is, advance work is a hugely important part of properly representing oneself, and failure to understand something so fundamental can be a serious detriment to the cause.

An advance is just another form of introduction. It's an icebreaker with venue representatives. It's the primary contact between artist and venue prior to your arrival, and it can set the tone for an entire relationship if handled, or not handled, properly.

Not every venue handles the advance the same way. At times it gets done with the talent buyer responsible for booking the engagement. Other times it's done with a manager, or general manager, of the concert facility itself. Then there are instances when it gets handled by a production manager or sound person who may or may not work directly for the venue. That all depends on the size of the venue and the way their business is structured. But regardless of the method employed by these venues, performing attractions should have their own system for gathering information as well.

Here are some basic suggestions which can help to facilitate the process:

- Make your initial outreach to the appropriate venue contact *at least a week prior to the performance date*, if not ten days or more. If the date is a part of a tour or extended number of shows, putting together a tour book which details each situation well in advance will ease the process on the road. But even if the event is a one-off situation, the further in advance you make your contact the greater the likelihood that any peculiarities or inconsistencies can be resolved prior to the performance date itself (which is often too late to fix any problems that might occur).
- Check out the venue Web site to get a feel for the space and see that the basic performance details listed match your notes.
- Create a checklist for yourself as a reminder of all the questions that need to be asked (see below).
- Always be polite and courteous to the person with whom you are dealing, even if that person does not reciprocate.
- Do not hesitate to make several calls if you are not receiving a call back.
- Do not assume that you have done your duty after leaving your first message or two, as if the burden of ensuring a quality performance is now in the hands of the venue contact. While that may seem reasonable and be partially correct in theory, it will not be considered a viable excuse if the performance does not go smoothly and will not be remembered when it's time to rebook.
- If after the third or fourth message you still don't get a call back, do not hesitate to go back to the person who booked the show and ask him or her if you have the correct info, and/or whether they can help to facilitate the process.
- If there are other artists performing on the same bill as yours, consider calling them too, to introduce yourself, talk about stage setup and equipment, and discuss the possibility of sharing gear to save time in transition between sets.

The most important thing to remember when doing an advance is this: Knowing prior to arrival the situation and the various players you'll encounter will minimize the surprises and allow you to focus on the performance itself. And an event without incident will be remembered—it may even be considered by some to be as important as the performance itself. This is especially true for an emerging artist who is trying to develop a good reputation and could use the support of as many people as will give it—including talent buyers, venue managers, production people, bartenders/wait staff, other performers, and fans alike.

For reference, an advance checklist should include the following, some of which will just be to reconfirm what has already been agreed:

Date
Venue name and address
Venue contact name, phone number, and e-mail address
Production/sound and lighting contact name, phone number, and e-mail address to reconfirm that they have the equipment you seek and know what equipment you will provide (i.e., ensure that they received your tech rider, which should include a stage plot and input list)
Name(s) of other act(s) on the bill, and related contact info
Directions
Parking
Load-in time(s)
Load-in situation (if there are stairs or elevators, if the loading area is on the front, side, or rear of the facility, if there are people to help, etc.)
Sound check time(s)
Door time
Set time(s)
Set length
Curfew
Deal/payment information (i.e., Who will handle payment? How much, when, and by what method? Do they have proper tax info? Was there a deposit?)
Merchandise (Who sells it? What's the split?)
Ticket price
Age limit (All ages, 16+, 18+, 21+)

Guest list size/number of complimentary tickets allotted
Dressing room situation (Is there one? Where? Does it have a bathroom/shower?)
Hospitality situation (meals, buyouts, beverages—alcoholic and non—towels, m&m's, etc.)
Availability of house backline (i.e., do they own amps and/or instruments you may wish to use?)
Stage size

These are the basics. They don't guarantee an event without incident—as the possibility remains that circumstances can change—but they increase the odds of all-around satisfaction and can help catch minor inconsistencies, which may not be minor after the fact. For instance, if an artist is to be paid by check, yet fails to advance his date and shows up on the day of show to find the check is made out to the wrong person, or if the check won't be available until however many days later because tax information wasn't supplied, whose fault is that? Artists often blame these oversights on the purchaser, their agent, or manager—yet a proper advance should have caught the mistake(s) in time to correct the problem. Isn't that reason enough to make sure everyone's on the same page?

Additional points of information that may arise from time to time—though they are typically addressed separately prior to the confirmation itself—include the radius clause,* advertising and promotional expectations, the sharing of press lists/contacts, and anything else that is unique to the artist and/or the venue (such as sponsorships and potential conflicts of interest) that the other party should know upon entering into a binding agreement.

Armed with all of the above information, you will do yourself proud and be set up for success. Your events will go more seamlessly, you will (typically) get paid on time, and people will respect and appreciate your professionalism. Now you just have to repeat this process every time you play!

* For those who don't know, a radius clause is a restriction that promoters often place on an artist which prohibits the artist from performing within a certain number of miles of the

venue for a certain number of days before and after, in order to protect his or her investment.

Always On the Clock

I once worked with a multicultural band that I believe to this day had the possibility to become great. They fused Caribbean, African, and American music; sang in six or seven languages; and had a punk-rock sensibility and style that made them unlike anything else. They were earning attention everywhere east of the Mississippi in the few years during which we had a business relationship. Unfortunately, the band had one member who couldn't keep his mouth shut.

This one member suffered from we-are-the-only-band-in-the-universe-that-matters disease. He just couldn't understand why they weren't the exception to every rule. He would walk around the venues with an air about him that suggested he honestly believed people were lucky to be in his presence. He was demanding of bartenders and wait staff, and he generally made a nuisance of himself.

In reality, he was an unbelievably gifted musician, and a little self-control in the short term probably would have led to the type of kid-gloves treatment he clearly felt he deserved. But unfortunately, it's simply irresponsible behavior for a young artist to assume he deserves the diva treatment. As in other facets of life, respect is something that must be earned, and in music you earn it by showing it first. Of course, he believed he showed it with his instrument and that great music was all that was required. But, in the end, his mouth did more damage than his instrument did good, because he failed to appreciate the simple concept that when building a following and developing a relationship with venues, an artist is always *on the clock*.

From the time of first contact, whether you are soliciting your services or doing your advance for a date, you are always on the clock. Upon arrival at each venue, each time you are there, even on nights

127

when you aren't performing, neither lapse in judgment nor letting down your guard is acceptable behavior.

Of course it is widely assumed that getting drunk and trashing rooms is considered cool and gets overlooked in rock 'n' roll. But, in reality, that is rarely the case for any band at any level, no matter what your stature—for at the end of the night someone will get an earful, and that band better be a big ticket seller if they want an invite back, just as they'd better have deep pockets to cover the damages they cause and be prepared to make amends as any decent human would do.

It should be obvious for any young artist hoping to break into the business that acting appropriate under all circumstances is imperative. Unfortunately, in the case of this band whose weak link caused great concern, this was a lesson they learned the hard way. One night, after absolutely killing it in Philadelphia, the aforementioned resident hothead got caught up in an argument with a bouncer. Though the reasons were unclear, he was forcibly removed from the club and effectively ended his band's relationship with that venue, in spite of the praise the performance received from the talent buyer the next afternoon.

Failure to demonstrate professionalism can manifest itself in many forms. Stealing beer is a popular one, trashing dressing rooms is another. Selling sodas you found in a storage closet located near the merchandising area takes guts but little brains. Showing up late is another common problem. Showing up ten minutes before your stage time—demanding that backline be provided for your seven-piece band when you were supposed to be performing solo—happens. Believe me, I've had the misfortune of working with bands that have done each of these things.

The music industry is small, so when something happens people know. When you act foolishly, or speak "out of school," or say something negative about another—odds are it will get around. Taken out of context, things can come off a whole lot worse than intended. But in any context there is really no place for this bad behavior.

Go about your business as if you were on any career path. Mind your manners, stay clear of wrongdoing, behave appropriately (however playful), and never forget your end game—because the fact is, you are *always* on the clock.

Always Be at Your Best Onstage

There is no acceptable excuse for a second-rate performance—neither to the fan or the casual observer, nor the members of your band or the other acts on the bill, nor the promoter or anyone else who has invested in what you do. Of course there will be nights that are better than others, by virtue of one circumstance or another. But the simple fact is that to be the best you must perform your best, consistently. In order to do that, you must aspire to put on the absolute best performance of your life, every time you take to the stage, never once accepting anything less than everything you've got.

Opines Chris Ross, bass player of the Australian band Wolfmother, echoing the sentiments of innumerable greats who have preceded him, "We put everything into our shows … You only get to do this once, so why not put everything into it and see what happens?"[3]

Neither sickness nor sadness nor whatever happens in your life—*nothing* should keep a performer from delivering the goods. I don't care whether there are ten people or ten thousand in the audience. When an artist takes to the stage: *that* is his or her moment to shine. When a young artist aspires to greatness (or even just to make a living), the time spent onstage should never be wasted under any circumstances.

Consider the stage an oasis—an astonishingly beautiful place where others only dream they could be. Performing is what musicians get paid to do, even when it isn't very much. It is what their fans (or prospective fans) have come to see, no matter how few of them there

---

3   Peters, Mitchell. "Wolfmother" *Pollstar*, 19 June 2006.

are. Let me put it simply: failure to pour one's heart and soul into every single note—however many excuses there may be—is a detriment to one's craft and disrespect to one's audience. Never forget that the health of the industry itself is reliant upon concertgoers consistently getting the most bang for their buck.

Remember this, all you musicians who grow tired of playing to small crowds: fans love to be among the first to discover a great new band. True music lovers and showgoers covet the opportunity to be there in the early days. They buy merchandise, talk about the band, and start their own grassroots campaign boasting to friends and fellow music lovers about their incredible find. The buzz that evolves simply through word of mouth about a band that puts their all into every single date is not to be undermined or overlooked. Thus, consistency is critical, as two of those ten people standing in the back of the room may very well have the capacity to jump-start your career. You never know who those people may be or what could happen as a result of their enthusiastic response! In other words, half-assed efforts produce half-assed results, and an audience won't grow if they're not buying what you're selling. But the bands that put everything into their performances are the ones that get the most out of it, and give themselves a chance.

To sweep fans off their feet and transport them to another place— to a place where the artist rules supreme, if only for a short time—that is what every performer should aspire to. If it isn't, you probably don't belong there in the first place. Think about what it is that inspires you, and convey that sentiment to your fans. Think back to those moments when you stood before your idols, and consider the possibility that the shoe is now on the other foot. The mind's eye of the artist is where the audience wants to be—it's a peek into an artist's heart and soul, and a fundamental reason why fans come to the show. *Give them what they want. That is your job.* Don't ever forget it, and please don't take it lightly. Anyone, in any vocation, who is given a platform on which to express themselves, should recognize the opportunity they've been given and seize it with all their might. *Give 100 percent effort, 100 percent of the time,* never forgetting how fortunate you are to get paid to do what millions of others do recreationally, simply for the love of music.

Section IV

Getting Closer

Hard Work Does Not Equal Success

The act of doing does not constitute fulfillment of a duty, nor does it ensure success. Leaving a message does not alleviate the need to follow through or put the onus on someone else, as if you've done all you need to do. Doing something to move your career in the right direction is all well and good—but it's only truly meaningful if you are doing the right things. There are always things that need to be done, and it's easy to get mired in the minutiae. With an overabundance of activities and a finite amount of time, doing a little of this and a little of that can feel like progress even when it is not.

Let's say you make a series of booking inquiries but can't seem to fill the dates. You are routing from Omaha, Nebraska, to Philadelphia, Pennsylvania, and have anchors in both places, plus a strong possibility in Chicago. But you need at least four or five more dates to justify the trip, and you just can't make them stick. Anyone who has ever booked a tour can relay stories of sleepless nights and heat flashes that occur when you awaken at 4:00 AM thinking, *Oh God—how am I ever going to fill February 21 between Nashville and DC?* If you fail, will the rest of the band care that you put forth the effort? *Thanks for what?* The old college try just isn't enough.

Perhaps you send a series of packages to venues and agents believing you are every music lover's dream, but you don't follow up effectively to ensure they give you a listen. Or worse, you solicit them blindly, without any knowledge of their process (or whether they accept blind solicitations in the first place), nor specific names to which the packages should be sent. Is this a good use of your time—never knowing whether they hear you, or what they think if they do, with no means of gathering feedback whatsoever? (See "Solicitation Dos and Don'ts" in Section III for more examples of how you can spend countless hours soliciting with no positive end result.) It's astonishing how much time is wasted when the wrong approach is employed.

There comes a point when mailing packages isn't enough, when you are trying to connect with seasoned veterans who care about more than being a good guy—just as there is a point when picking up gigs for the sake of it isn't enough, when running through material doesn't make it better, and when putting the hours in at the office doesn't get the job done right because you are operating in a vacuum and failing to see the big picture. Perhaps your street team isn't focused and functions more as a support network than a vehicle to promote the band. Maybe your target demographic is slightly older than you think, because 1980s-inspired rock may be coming back again but not when you sound like Mister Mister. No matter how many of your friends say your song belongs on the radio, it does not necessarily mean you should solicit program directors nationwide—especially when the song is nine minutes long.

In a business with no clearly defined career path, success can't always be measured in tangibles. For a young band it may be as simple as a great tour which doesn't lose money, or surpassing one hundred paid attendance for the very first time. With so much to do, completing each task is the only way to evaluate progress and enjoy the fruits of your labor. Unfortunately, however, having a strong work ethic isn't enough to ensure that you realize those incremental achievements, even when they seem small in the grand scheme. For hard work does not always equal success, but if you do work hard to do all of the right things it just might give you the opportunity to have success down the road.

Three in a Million

I have a theory that three in every million artists and aspiring professionals "make it" in the music industry:[4]

One artist makes it because his or her talent is so great that it cannot be denied. You see him or her and you just know. Whether it has happened yet or will soon enough, there is no doubt in your mind.

One gets "lucky." It's not that his or her talent would not result in success over time—for the potential is certainly there—it's just that somehow there are those who question how it happened when it did.

One makes it the old-fashioned way: through tireless effort, working all hours of the day, pursuing all angles, and following all leads, both on and offstage.

Odds are that you, the reader, do not fall into Category A. If you did, you probably wouldn't be reading this book. Odds are you do not fall into Category B either. You might, as we will talk about shortly what it takes to become lucky, but the odds nevertheless do not change. In fact, odds are you do not fall into Category C either, for three in a million is not a favorable ratio, no matter who you are.

If you have been a musician for a number of years, performing recreationally in small to mid-size soft ticket venues (the ones where a good band and a good crowd collide, but the crowd is not necessarily there for that band specifically), then it's probably safe to say you do

---

4   By using a quick calculation, dividing the world population and a generalized conception of how many artists succeed (whatever your definition of success may be), you'll discover that I am speaking metaphorically.

not fall into Categories A or B, no matter how much talent you possess. Therefore, Category C is your only real shot.

On the other hand, those who have only been performing for a short while may believe that they could still fall into one of the first two groups. But then, why spend the next several years of your life just hoping that proves the case? Why hold out for the possibility that someone will come along who is willing and able to make it happen for you, rather than using your time effectively to increase your odds of success on your own terms?

Of course, it is ultimately about the music—for most, anyway. So focusing on the music first makes great sense, and believing you possess superior talent is of tremendous value. However, in the music business, both the music and the business need to function at the very highest levels in order for an artist to truly achieve success beyond his or her wildest dreams. So make your music great. But be mindful and considerate of the business elements as well, to increase the odds that you too may become one of just three in a million.

The Closer You Get, the Further It Seems

In the early months and years, there are so many broad concepts requiring attention that the little things often get overlooked—and with good reason. Performance isn't crisp? No big deal—better just to get through the show, keep the energy level high, and make some connection with the crowd. Recording isn't radio-ready? That's okay—better to capture the raw emotion of the material. There is any number of elements which could be improved, but taking the small victories as they come is so much more important—until things start coming together, and that's when it starts to get hard.

It feels great when signs of progress become evident and people start to notice. You feel like you are starting to get close. But that's when things get flipped—when you discover that the closer you get the further it seems, and you realize the devil is in the details.

It's no longer acceptable that a show is really good. Good is not good enough. It has to be great, *every time*.

It just doesn't cut it that the venue *almost* sells out—you should aspire to sell it out in advance, *every night*.

The band *has* to be tight. The audience *has* to keep growing. The record *has* to be the best re-creation of the music possible, and one about which you can feel proud for years to come.

Industry insiders are notoriously skeptical of everything that crosses their desk. Fans become increasingly insistent that their favorite bands present themselves just so. Once big dollars enter the equation—or the hint thereof comes into play—then it becomes an absolute imperative that every *i* gets dotted and every *t* gets crossed.

In the chapter on "Practice Does Not Make Perfect" I referred to a pop band I worked with a few years back. I believe they serve as a good example in this context as well. Frustrating though they turned out to be, on the surface they seemed to have a good thing going when I first got involved. They had a manager who believed in them, they had the requisite "business guy" in the band who served as their point person, and they designated assignments among the members pretty well.

They'd been together for about four years when I took them on and there was talk that a "deal" was not far off. Without question, they were THE band about town in Boston. We set out to build their local fan base even bigger. We started testing new markets, and, though the draw was inconsistent, they were doing solid numbers in a few places. We also introduced them to the college scene and people responded well, which kept a steady amount of money flowing in.

They did many of the little things well. Their street team had its deficiencies, but the troops certainly worked hard. They ran promotions for fans to win one thing or another and it kept spirits high. They had some interpersonal differences, but they were able to work through them—until slowly things came to a head.

I'd been with them for a couple of years when they asked me to join them for a band meeting one night. It may have been my idea—I do not recall. All I know is that the meeting was long overdue. They had a new record on the horizon, and there was a sense that this was "it"—they were starting to feel the weight of their promise and they were starting to point fingers at one another behind each other's backs, insinuating, "That's why we aren't there yet."

As we sat around their studio, we discussed the value of making a renewed commitment to each other: that if, indeed, this was to be the final push, then they should agree to go all out for one full year, watching each other's backs, picking one another up when they fell down, and putting their respective best foot forward in everything that they did. Then, after the year each one would reassess. Everyone agreed without hesitation. The positive energy in the room was palpable.

Then, the decision was made to talk about the areas in which each of them wanted to see improvement, and that's when the cracks in the seam began to appear.

"You need to work on your keyboard parts."

"Yeah, well you need to come to rehearsal with a better attitude."

"You aren't pulling your weight."

"Yeah, well your weight is becoming a problem."

(*Please note: I am paraphrasing, as I do not recall the exact words exchanged, but each of these sentiments and so many more made their way to the surface over the course of the next hour or so ...)

In prior years, when it had all been about fun, the band members rarely concerned themselves with the inconsequential details. There were whispers about one member who drank too much before the shows, and another who clearly was the least talented musician in the group. There was one member who didn't fit the mold of a pop band, because a lead guitarist is supposed to be the "cool guy" and not the heavyset kid who stands in the back. But none of those things seemed to matter much—at least not to the point where resolution was an overwhelming concern.

Perhaps if they'd stuck it out and continued to work as a team with a common cause rather than turning on one another—which is what happened about halfway through their one-year agreement—the "deal" that they sought would have come. But that was not meant to be for this crew.

The swan song for the lead singer (and me, as a result) came on a cool November night in 2005, when they did fifteen hundred people headlining Boston's Avalon Ballroom—more people than most unsigned bands ever do. Yet that was the end for these guys. Sure, the rest of the band attempted to carry on with a replacement singer for another year or so, but the fire was gone. There is no telling just how close they came. All I know is that when they were there it seemed so far away.

I'm not suggesting a band must be at its peak in order to break big in the business. Quite the contrary—the entire organization must continue to evolve over the course of a band's lifespan in order to enjoy the staying power that keeps an act relevant in the landscape of popular culture. Nor am I saying they must have it all figured out and resolve all their issues before the break comes along. Rather, I suggest all artists be resolute in their quest to work through their kinks, but always to keep them in perspective and never lose sight of their shared objective, whatever that may be.

That said, what better reason is there to start getting organized now than the knowledge that one day those minor details will matter?

For when they do, you will want to have a plan to make everything right and to continue making progress—rather than being faced with the overwhelming mountain of details to be improved upon and risk getting crushed under the weight. That is, if you are so fortunate as to know what they are.

Luck

The harder I work, the luckier I get.

—golfer Gary Player

Luck is what happens when preparation meets opportunity

—Chinese fortune cookie

Some people rise to prominence faster than others—there is no denying the fact. It happens in every facet of life. While one person struggles for everything he or she achieves, the next person seems to have everything handed to him or her on a silver platter. Often we refer to the latter person as being *lucky*. He or she appears to *have it made*. There's not necessarily any one answer to why that may be—it just *is*.

Sometimes people achieve because they have a strong work ethic. Sometimes people achieve because they have greater opportunity, whether due to their background, or means, or any number of reasons related to gender, wealth, good looks, intelligence, or—not to be overlooked—talent.

It may be raw, it may be polished, it may come naturally, it may take hard work—and it may take all of the above.

It may also take time, or it could happen quickly—there is really no timetable one can set. As noted previously, Maroon5 took several years before they exploded internationally. Yet thanks to *American Idol*, Kelly Clarkson rocketed to fame in a matter of months, or so it would seem.

Whatever the circumstances, however success comes, the ultimate fallacy in the music industry is the notion that luck is the difference between stardom and obscurity. Now, that's not to say there aren't exceptions to the rule—the phrase *one in a million* comes from somewhere. But the majority of us have to work our tails off to earn the opportunity to "get lucky," and that's really the long and short of it. So get past the pipe dream, roll up your sleeves, and accept the fact that you're going to have to work for a living, because that is just how it gets done.

It takes countless hours of study, practicing your craft—whether writing, performing, reading, or recording. You can't become a doctor or a lawyer overnight. You don't earn promotions or the respect of your peers without something to back it all up. So then, what makes you think Britney Spears was a fluke? Or that 'NSync could have been any old bunch? Sure they've been lucky, if by lucky you mean fortunate, but make no mistake—no accident occurred. It's always the pop stars that I hear people think happened purely by dumb luck. Sure, they may not have followed the steps outlined in this book; they may have been in the right place at the right time and won an audition or got spotted in a talent show. So maybe they are that one-in-a-million star that doesn't have to work for it the way the rest of us do. But that doesn't necessarily mean that it was all just dumb luck.

Let's not overlook that something special which entertainers possess—the *it* factor, as we will discuss shortly. Let's not be so shortsighted as to believe luck is the only thing they've got going for them. Sure, people win the lottery all the time. An elderly woman may play the same number her entire life and can't believe that she finally hits big when she's eighty-four. It gives us all hope and makes us hold on to the belief that anything is possible. But for every lottery winner there are tens of millions more of us who must work to realize our dreams. Those of us who do are fortunate indeed—lucky, if you will—to have persevered, to have developed our craft by honing our skills over the course of many years, until finally we are given the opportunity to be successful—and when that day comes we call ourselves lucky.

Time to Take a Chance

This one goes out to the singer/songwriters above all.

As the fan base grows to include more than just the casual concertgoer, so too should the length and variety of the performance in a headline situation. Similarly, as time goes by and your confidence swells, you will start to feel that the stage is your home. When that day comes, no longer will it be necessary to employ the fast-and-furious approach to serving up middle-of-the-road numbers aimed at getting the audience up on their feet in hopes that they will create an infectious energy that will carry you through to the end. Rather, the time will come when it's better to try new things and take a chance on the songs that you may have previously been wise to avoid.

I worked with a wonderful singer/songwriter named CP for a couple of years who I believe will have a lasting career if he works at it. But I often found myself pleading with him to introduce some of the more emotionally challenging numbers into his sets, believing his fans were yearning to hear them. One song in particular is about him standing beside a dying relative, and I always believed it was his single best piece of work. I never blamed him for shying away from such a track in favor of the lighter pop fare that he served up well and aplenty. But I have never stopped believing it would have catapulted him further and faster, as the emotion on his sleeve was always well received, and in my mind there comes a time when you've got to take that chance.

You, the musician, need to make your listeners feel as you feel—or felt on a particular day—even if you are forced to relive those emotions over and again on the stage before an audience that you don't really know. Share those moments in time to which they can relate, and know in your heart that they will give something equally powerful back to you. Recall the Springsteen quote (Section III: Performance Techniques) about the relationship between performer and audience.

Around the same time that I was working with CP I was also handling RJ, the singer/songwriter referenced in "Time to Burst the Bubble." Unlike CP, RJ took the opposite approach to his performance. Every song was so heartfelt you got an emotional workout every time that he came to town. While his fan base has not grown beyond the tipping point, he has pockets of fans who live and breathe for his shows, as if he were delivering religious rituals to the faithful each time, always lifting them up and never once letting them down. Sadly, his fault (as previously discussed, in my opinion) was not his failure to take a chance but his inability (or, in some cases, his refusal) to do all the other things. Nevertheless, I often suggest to young singer/songwriters that they see him and experience for themselves what it means to take a chance.

The bottom line is: Your fans may love every lyric delivered with a straightforward pop rock sensibility—and that may well be your bread and butter for the entirety of your career. But if you just take a chance every once in a while, you might surprise some people, and increase your opportunity to win over new fans (not to mention keep the old ones coming back). Who knows—you might even surprise yourself.

What It Is All About

There are a number of variables that determine the success of an artist in the music business of the twenty-first century, any one of which is arguably the most important of all.

It's All About the Music

You may spend your days and nights as if you're the only one in the universe: not caring what anyone thinks; not bothering to network with your contemporaries, nor showing any interest in understanding the process; not working your audience when you take to the stage, nor working the crowd when you finish your set; not doing any of the things that common sense dictates you should to build your career and get yourself to a better place. If you write great songs, or record a brilliant album that just happens to fall into the right hands, then none of those factors necessarily matter, and the rest may take care of itself.

So forget about writing that inspiring bio or taking that cool press photo. Be the antibusiness type of musician, if you like. Just pour your heart and soul into that record. There is really nothing else that you are required to do. Leave the rest to someone else if that's what you prefer, and remind yourself that the business sucks the life out of the music, and that's not what you are about.

You are an artist. Great art speaks for itself. So let your music stand on its own. It doesn't really matter what anyone else thinks. At the end of the day, it's all about the music.

It's All About Entertainment

You may act like a clown or a drunken buffoon; you might not know how to play your own instrument. You might piss off venue managers everywhere you perform. You might make obscene gestures to your audience. You could write songs with no point, void of all substance or expression. Your album could be absolute shit. Yet you could become a big star. For you are a part of the entertainment industry.

So forget about the business. Who cares about the music? If you can entertain then your audience they will love you for it, and everything else can take care of itself. Leave great songs to the next band, that needn't be what defines you.

You are an entertainer—that's what you do. And great entertainment is something people want and need to escape from their lives every once in a while.

So be who you are, no matter what that may be. Whether people are mesmerized by your talent or the train-wreck factor applies, you may become a great success, because, at the end of the day, it's all about entertainment.

It's All About the Business

The music is a given, whatever your sound may be. Your entertainment value is just another element. You may or may not put the asses in the seats, but that's of little consequence yet. For you have a business plan, and that's more than most bands can say.

You have common sense; you know there's a process which every business must follow, and a rock band is no different than the rest. Just because you don't sit behind a desk in a suit doesn't mean the same rules don't apply, so you will do what you must do to achieve.

You are a business person. You understand that in the music business it takes both. You have a plan, and you know how to execute. You know who and what you are; you have a philosophy about what you do. You make strategic alliances, and you have a vision for the future.

You have figured out how to build a base that starts with your friends, but it ultimately requires you to make fans. You are aware that ultimately you aren't going to recognize every face in the crowd if you want to succeed. So you invite your friends—everyone you can find—

to your shows every time! And you persuade them to come back, and they bring their friends, who bring theirs, and theirs, and so on. Then you work up a strategy to maximize record sales by locating key people who pass them around, burn them, upload them, download them, and so on—whatever works and gets you where you want to go.

However you build your empire, whatever steps that you take, if you meet your goals and objectives, then you will find the success you deserve. You will earn it through blood, sweat, and tears. And it will feel good. For you know something that most never learn: that at the end of the day, it's all about the business.

It's All About Asses in Seats

Your music may be garbage, not a lick worth a journalist's note. You might look at the floor while you play, believing your audience is not worth acknowledgment. You might resent the notion that you are an entertainer, like a marionette on strings, or a trained monkey, or an actor playing a role. You are just you, and that's all that you are, and for whatever reason (none that anyone else can define), you happen to be a great success. For at the end of the day, no matter what you may hear, as a touring musician there's just one way to pay the bills.

So forget about the music. What does it matter what anyone else thinks? If you can sell tickets, then agents will come out of the woodwork, labels and managers will call, slots and trades will be offered, and touring opportunities will soon follow. You can survive in the cutthroat music business—you have what it takes—because at the end of the day, barring everything else, it's all about asses in seats.

What Is Your Story?

The aforementioned variables which define an artist's success may be interconnected or may have no commonalities at all. A sound argument can be made for each of them, as there is truth in every one.

Great art may or may not be the difference-maker—who hears it and what catches on is never guaranteed. But when the right people put their stamp of approval on a project it can make all the difference, no matter what else you do. So a great record can in fact catapult an artist from obscurity to superstardom.

Even more likely than a record finding the right ear is the fact that a great entertainer will almost inevitably garner attention. If you can win people over with charisma and charm, in-your-face behavior, comedic timing, or by any other means, then you will stand out, separate from the rest. In spite of certain musical deficiencies, good things may very well come to those who entertain.

That said, barring an impressive musical prowess or a great stage presentation, a great business plan and a matching work ethic can nevertheless manufacture a profitable venture. Perhaps you capitalize on a recognizable brand—perhaps a movie character or a theme. You may write songs about your favorite sneaker then launch a grassroots marketing campaign which generates attention by virtue of association. These things happen from time to time. Check out the song "Vans" by a group called The Pack.

On the other hand, perhaps you have achieved a level of celebrity as a model or actor, a socialite or a scenester, or simply on account of a unique background which people find appealing. You may find that people come out of the woodwork to see what you will do next. Maybe it's decent, perhaps not really. Even a total train wreck can have a positive end result, as sometimes it really *is* all about asses in seats. If people are willing to pay the price of admission, regardless of any reasonable explanation why—at least not with respect to what you do on stage—you still may realize a level of success far beyond all expectations.

The point is, any one of these assets can lead to success in spite of the absence of another. Each element which you possess helps craft the story which helps people identify who you are and what you represent—gives you a hook, if you will. An interesting story with many facets will inevitably garner greater attention. Therefore, I submit that it makes considerably more sense to work on each of these areas rather than to focus on just one, thereby increasing the odds that *at least one of them* will make the difference for you.

The Real Deal

Whatever it is that makes you special—whoever you are or are trying to be, perhaps the most important thing to keep in mind when entering the business of making music is that it's never entirely about you. It is always about the fans.

It is their connection to you, whatever the attraction may be, that allows the relationship to bloom. It could be something about the music you write or the way you convey your emotions on stage. It could be something about your background; where you come from or your environment or family. It could be something seemingly insignificant to you that makes all the difference to them. Whatever it is, *that* is what really matters. *That* is why all of the techniques discussed throughout this collection are written with the fans in mind.

Section V

When the Stars Align

The It Factor

It cannot be defined by any tangible means—it just is. When a boisterous crowd in an otherwise noisy bar is reduced to a hush, *it* has happened. When an infectious energy overtakes an audience and sends them into a frenzy, *it* has happened. When the show is over and no one wants to go because life in the moments just past is what living is all about, *it* has happened. The *it* factor is oft spoken about but rarely understood. So it begs the question: What is *it*?

When an attractive woman walks into the room, heads turn. Whether you like her or not, she captures your attention. But what makes her attractive? Perhaps *it*'s her eyes, her smile, her style, or her way. *It* could be one of these things, or none of these things—*it* is what stands out in the eye of the beholder, because *it* isn't a universal truth, as not everyone responds to the same stimuli. But regardless, *it* evokes a reaction.

It is something, anything that draws one to another. *It* could be the way the singer holds the microphone, the way the guitarist struts across the stage, or the way the drums make your heart beat in time. *It* could have something to do with the songwriting, or the swagger, or the rhythm, or anything that moves you to *feel.* Some performers have it all: the way they sing, the way they dance, whatever. On the other hand, some have just one stand-out quality that you can point to. But whatever *it* is, it is enough, because *it* engages the audience in a transcendental way.

People talk about "the hook" being what makes a song, whether it be the chorus, the guitar line, the bridge, or the break. Similarly, the *it* factor is like the hook applied to an overall performance. *It* is magnetism.

Some people have *it*, some people don't. Some are born with *it*, others develop *it* over time. Whether *it* can be learned or just happens I really can't say. But I know *it* when I see *it*, and so do others. When *it* happens, people want to be around *it*, and good things follow. So whatever it is that's deep inside you could be *it*, if not now, then in time. So nurture it, foster it, and perhaps you'll attain *it*, and that's when things will really start to happen.

Overnight Success?

The notion that popular artists appear out of nowhere—as·if plucked from obscurity and given the national stage, with the world at their fingertips in what appears to be an instant, and everything they ever dreamed of hand-delivered on a platter—is a fantastic concept in theory, and something many would love to believe is real. But in truth, it is nothing more than an exaggeration in terms, propagated by the mass media.

Certainly it makes for great copy, and the *American Idol* series milks this concept for all that it's worth. But short of winning a talent contest that promises international superstardom, most popular artists—even the great ones—spend years honing their craft before making the leap and achieving the notoriety that seemingly transcends space and time.

Consider the example of Maroon5, as referred to in the chapter "Don't Quit Your Day Job." To win a Grammy for Best New Artist ten years into a career says a lot about the commitment required to break through in the music industry, and even more about what happens when a song breaks through at radio, propelling the career of a touring band and taking them under the radar to critical mass.

Plain White T's provides similar context. The band first formed in the late 1990s, and signed its first label deal to Atlantic in 2000. But three labels, four records, and six years of touring later, the band was all but unknown to most of the world until "Hey There Delilah" took off on radio in 2007.

The same holds true with the Gym Class Heroes. Formed in 1997, they released five records and toured consistently for eight years before they had their first hit with "Cupid's Chokehold" on the *As Cruel as School Children* album. That recognition finally propelled them to the national stage and earned them the 2007 title Best New Artist awarded by MTV (similar to that which Maroon5 earned by the Grammys in their—perhaps not coincidental—tenth year as a band).

Of course, there are exceptions to every rule. Consider the story of Colbie Caillat—who didn't even pick up an instrument until she turned nineteen years old, yet by twenty-two was a hitmaker thanks to the song "Bubbly," which catapulted her into the national spotlight, in spite of being unsigned, after she posted it on *MySpace*. Ms. Caillat may actually be the closest thing to a true overnight success, and proof positive that all things are possible, thanks in large part to the social networking possibilities afforded by the Internet. Of course, in the case of Ms. Caillat it remains to be quantified just how significant a role her father played; he coproduced the Fleetwood Mac classic album *Rumours*.

Of greater consequence are the nagging questions which accompany such a rapid advancement through the ranks. For instance, how does an overnight success story handle the big stage, without the years of experience developing a level of comfort as the size of the crowds increases? Also, are the listeners and concertgoers actual fans of the artist or just the hit song? And if the latter is the case, what happens after the song cycle inevitably runs its course? Without the foundation that can only come from years of mining the trenches, building true fans one at a time, the answers to these questions do not necessarily spell long-lasting success.

Nevertheless, it is clear there is truth in the notion that a hit song can transform an artist's career overnight. In fact, it would seem that a hit song transforms every artist's career overnight, taking them from wherever they were to wherever they go. So perhaps the point isn't so much about what a hit song can do, but rather about what artists have done to prepare themselves for what comes next, and whether they continue to grow or slowly fade away.

To that end, I submit that a more realistic example of an artist whose *career* really took off in a short period of time, without benefit of radio, is one of my personal favorites: Robert Randolph. Here is a young man who grew up playing the pedal steel in the House of God Church until a series of introductions dating from the spring of 2000 led to a gig at the Bowery Ballroom, where he opened for the North Mississippi Allstars. That break, and the exposure it brought Mr.

Randolph, led to a succession of performances that built the base which bore witness to what became his debut release, *Live at the Wetlands,* in the fall of 2001.

His is a remarkable talent that illustrates the possibility that overnight success, and a resulting career, are possible without a hit song—if an eighteen-month ascension to headlining four-hundred-capacity clubs can be called an overnight success—it takes a rare talent in the right place at the right time (see the chapter entitled "Luck") to be afforded such an opportunity. Of course, to this day, (at the time of printing in 2008), Randolph & his Family Band are neither a platinum-selling attraction nor a household name. Rather, he is merely comfortably entrenched in the modern music culture, touring alongside some of the greats, from Dave Matthews to Eric Clapton, doing what he loves to do.

So what then defines an overnight success? Several years later Robert Randolph has yet to achieve critical mass—where everyone immediately identifies his music and recognizes his name. I leave that definition to the individual. Of greater consequence to me is rendering false the notion that success is something that should happen in a matter of months simply because that is the way an artist believes it should be. There is a certain transcendence that naturally occurs when a song gets picked up by commercial radio or takes off via the Internet and within months takes an artist from hobbyist to superstar—but in only the most rare of instances was that hobbyist someone who'd been sitting around the house waiting for something to happen rather than slugging it out in the streets, in the clubs, and on tour. More than likely, the "overnight" success that most perceive was the result of someone's continual effort to position him or herself for future success, doing the little things with the help of a great support network.

Once again may I reference the book *The Tipping Point* by Malcolm Gladwell and strongly suggest that you read it. I could not make the point any better myself of how trends evolve and spread when placed in the hands of "Connectors, Mavens, and Salesmen." They may be major music industry players, in front of or behind the scenes, or even just an undeniably effective group of friends or fans who are capable of spreading the word in a manner which persuades people to do as they say and experience for themselves the power that a talented artist may possess. Whoever they may be, going to great lengths to identify and convert them, and get them to work for you, is imperative. But that takes time—both to find them and for them to do what they do—as few things happen overnight. But when it does happen it may appear to the casual observer to occur in an instant. However, you and I will know different.

Agents and Managers and Labels (Oh My!)

It isn't entirely fair that only one chapter out of so many is dedicated to agents and managers and labels—not to mention the numerous other role players who are getting no mention at all. But breaking into the business doesn't necessarily require any of the above in the early stages—in fact, I hope I've been clear that I frown upon jumping into any of these situations too soon. But in the event that an act is so fortunate that they have developed a certain stature all on their own and have earned a place at the metaphorical table, where the industry professionals go to drool over the "next big thing" (which is not so soon as most artists like to think, but nevertheless one day down the road) then it's important to choose wisely the people with whom you surround yourself. So how does one go about making those tough choices?

In the ever-changing music industry the answer unfortunately becomes less and less clear. There was a time when there were but a few roads to take, when everyone performing at Woodstock knew one another because they were it, as majors artists of the time went, and there were just a few major players in each of the major categories who could truly take an artist to the top. But over the years the number of agencies, management companies, and labels has increased, along with the ever-increasing number of artists who fall into conventional and niche categories. Can you imagine if such a festival existed in the twenty-first century, where every major artist on the planet performed over the course of a four-day weekend?

No longer is it necessarily the "right thing to do" to go and sign with CAA or William Morris when they come calling. Of course, if they do come calling you are most fortunate and might want to take that chance. But the ever-growing number of independent agencies, management firms, and labels is overwhelming, to say the least. As technology advances, so too does the number of outlets to distribute your music and make a living in the business you love, which begs the question: why sign the deal at all?

Of course, the arguments abound that the industry will soon crash, as the model cannot stand under its own weight for much longer—that the lack of artist development coupled with the saturation in the market (and of the senses) will one day blow up in the face of the "cash-in-now" generation. But in the end, that only reinforces the purpose of this book and leads me to one simple suggestion when you are making choices: whatever the need an artist has to fulfill—whether an agent, manager, label, et al.—common sense dictates that the best choices available will be the most passionate people, the people who possess the qualifications and have a plan that includes both long-terms goals and short-term objectives, which lead to the promise of a career—not stardom, per se, but actually living doing what it is that you love. If the effort is tireless and the talent is true—then, with time, energy, and common sense above all, following the simple guidelines that I've suggested, not to the letter of the law but to the laws of one's conscience—then it can happen. It's as simple as that. In no way does this suggest that every plan leads to the promised land, for the fact remains that most never will.

Recall the sentiment of the famed Hunter S. Thompson quote ("The Notion of the Big, Bad Industry"), and be cautious in the decisions you make. Just knowing there is a hint of that mentality in the industry only reinforces the importance of understanding the business and the value of a reality check every once in a while, before you sign with anyone at all.

Click! The Moment Arrives

You have finally arrived at the long-anticipated moment in time when the band feels like it's firing on all cylinders! The music is strong, the performance is tight, and the business is getting done because everyone is pulling their weight. The audiences are growing, the CDs are selling, and the opportunities are coming in—some are even completely unsolicited. The industry is taking notice. You are starting to feel like something good is really happening—not like before, when you relished each little victory. I mean, something is evidently happening, and the hobby which you have for years considered a career, in spite of what your critics all said, may actually evolve into a full-time vocation. Then you get the deal.

Not a deal—*the* deal. It's not the first thing that comes along—the one where you are not fully satisfied, but you feel compelled to sign anyway, because, what if it's the only one? What if this is it, and you don't get another shot? A lot of bands find themselves in that very position—or at least that's what they believe.

But I'm not talking about the mercy contract. I am talking about the one you've been waiting for. It could be a major-label record contract, or the hip new indie with whom you've dreamed of working. It might not be a label deal; it could be a distribution deal, or a 360/ profit sharing/multifaceted deal (ref: Korn, Madonna, Paramore), or, it could be just the right management contract. Whichever it is, this metaphoric deal, it is *the* dream; it is what you had hoped would happen sooner or later, after you painstakingly passed on the mercy deal, overcoming your own conscience and the members of the band

161

who said, "Fuck it—let's take what we can get ..." But you were clear that it wasn't worth your time, and you were prepared to stick to your guns, and that's exactly what you did, and—lo and behold—your instincts have actually paid off!

You withstood the Three Ps, you learned how to play the game, and you have reached the point where, "*Click!* The moment arrives." You have finally reached the elusive moment in time where you actually have the opportunity to succeed. It's not because of the deal. The deal is just a bank loan from someone who is ready to invest in whatever it is that you do. But the deal does have significance; it is symbolic of your progress and a positive sign that you are no longer alone—that someone out there actually believes in you and appreciates what you bring to the table.

You are at the point where you may choose your own destiny—not that you haven't chosen your own path up until now. But what's different now is the possibility to make your dreams a reality. You have set yourself up for success, and you finally have that opportunity. But let's back that up just a step and be clear about what exactly that means. The opportunity to succeed is not success in and of itself—it's just sea level, as discussed way back in the beginning. It's ground zero. Up until now you've been learning to swim in the shallow end of a pool, because there's no sense in jumping headfirst into the ocean if you can't do a lap in three and a half feet of water. But now you can swim back and forth in the pool. Well, that still doesn't qualify you for the Olympics—so let's not get too carried away. There is still so much work to do.

You have overcome many obstacles, and you should be proud, as you've come further than most ever will. But there is still a long way before you can live out your dreams, for the deal is nothing more than the next phase in the game. The deal itself is a platform—a life preserver if you will. With it you may take a moment to pause and reflect, and decide by what means, and with whom you will walk, or swim, as you enter a new arena and effectively start all over again—except this time you are taking what you know, which gives you the confidence to do what you will, as you go from being a big fish in a small pond to being a minnow in the sea.

So the process begins anew. But fortunately, this time it feels more like a continuation, and if you choose wisely you'll be glad to have additional layers of support. So choose wisely. Swim with the fish that you trust, not because they are necessarily the biggest, but because they complement your best attributes. And be prepared to work even harder than before—for now is not the time to get cocky and slack off. Be proud, but be mindful that the expectations are now greater, since others are investing time and money into you. You finally have a chance. You've beat those three-in-a-million odds. Enjoy it—and good luck. Your moment has arrived. You have earned the opportunity to succeed.

Conclusion

Over the course of this journey you will take as you foray deeper into the music business, I hope you will refer back to this book now and then. Perhaps you will follow the road map outlined step by step, through all the mental preparations, the business routines and exercises, the methods for exposing yourself and your craft, and the increased value that results from educating yourself about the process. Perhaps you have determined that my way is not for you, but you will extract bits and pieces that make more sense to your personal circumstances and that's that.

On the other hand, maybe all I've done is reinforce what you already know, giving you the confidence to do it on your own because you were already thinking the same thing, and it helps to know others feel exactly the same way. Positive reinforcement is an essential component of trusting your own common sense, and if I have helped just a little bit I am very proud.

Much like a record producer, whose responsibility is to bring out the best in his clients, I have always maintained that my mission is to help artists and aspiring music industry professionals fulfill their potential on the stage and in business. Hopefully that fulfillment carries over into their daily lives to the point that they feel compelled to do the same for others.

I do not profess to have all the answers, but I believe in my heart that a better-educated, more well-rounded, more prepared young artist and industry aspirant will go further in the end. If, by working together, we in the industry can help those coming in while they still are young and impressionable, then the end result will be a stronger music industry on the whole. That means better talent, both onstage and off, better ideas coming to light, and better ways of doing things (I don't claim to know what they are—just that there are people who do know if we give them the proper tools). These will all help to increase the bottom line.

Not only do I believe such improvements will increase sales of tickets and music, I believe they can also translate to the system of education in schools—better music and more educated musicians will ultimately remind people of the importance of arts education.

Arts education is critical in the development of future generations! It helps to expand the mind and provides the building blocks to succeed, not just in music, should they so desire, but more importantly to succeed in life. Working with others to raise the bar, to build a better music industry, and improve arts education in schools—that is my big dream.

Postscript: The Evolution of an Industry

As the industry moves further into the twenty-first century, a dramatic shift in the industry's paradigm from the major corporations to the individual is taking place, thanks in large part to the technological advancements which empower individuals by increasing the level of their control over their own destiny. An artist or aspiring industry professional no longer requires the assistance of a major label, management firm, agency, or publisher to expose his or her craft to the world. Whether you are creating a new technology or simply benefiting from the ease with which you can take advantage of one that already exists, the possibilities are endless. You can literally go as far as you want to go and do whatever it is that you aspire to do, no longer requiring the permission of a benefactor (i.e., a label or promoter), who under the old paradigm would have had a say, perhaps even control over your output, not to mention having taken a substantial piece of the action.

Furthermore, as the new technologies develop, opportunities to improve upon them—to do things that might or might not have previously been forecasted or foreseen—will continue the evolutionary process for the betterment of the industry as a whole. Artists will find new ways to connect with their fans, and those that take advantage will find themselves comfortably entrenched in an industry which might have seemed so unlikely and so far away just a few years ago. Today's music industry is wide open. The artists themselves possess power like never before, as do their fans—who are not to be overlooked—and not just a select few industry executives and the content of their quarterly reports.

Of course, I do not mean to imply that the execs with the big dollars and the decades of experience should be ignored. No, their knowledge and reach is still of substantial value, so in no way do I mean to suggest that they have become superfluous. Rather, they are still capable of taking you to new heights. Only now, armed with the knowledge which enables you to succeed on your own, you may join them as strategic partners and not just as subservient pawns in their game. Together we will take the industry into the twenty-second century, stronger and smarter than ever.

Printed in the United States
139528LV00001B/200/P